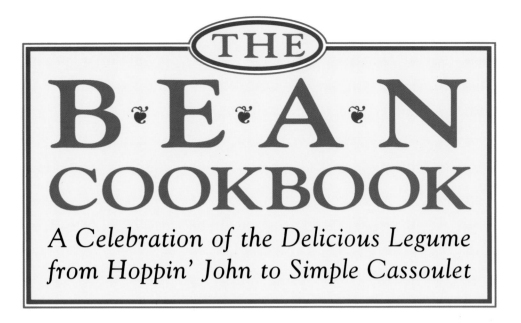

THE B·E·A·N COOKBOOK

A Celebration of the Delicious Legume from Hoppin' John to Simple Cassoulet

JUDITH CHOATE

PRINCIPAL PHOTOGRAPHY BY PETER JOHANSKY

FOOD STYLING BY DYNE BENNER

SIMON & SCHUSTER

London   Sydney   New York   Tokyo   Toronto   Singapore

A KENAN BOOK

Copyright © 1992 Kenan Books, Inc.
Text copyright Judith Choate

Simon & Schuster
Simon & Schuster Building
Rockefeller Center
1230 Avenue of the Americas
New York, New York 10020

SIMON & SCHUSTER and colophon are registered trademarks of Simon & Schuster Inc.

THE BEAN COOKBOOK
was prepared and produced by
Kenan Books, Inc.
15 West 26th Street
New York, New York 10010

Editor: Sharon Kalman
Art Director/Designer: Robert W. Kosturko
Photography Editor: Anne K. Price
Production Director: Karen L. Greenberg

1 3 5 7 9 10 8 6 4 2

Library of Congress Cataloging-in-Publication Data

Choate, Judith.
    The bean cookbook / Judith Choate.
        p.   cm.
    Includes bibliographical references and index.
    ISBN 0-671-73549-7
    1. Cookery (Beans)   I. Title.
  TX803.B4C46   1992
641.6′565—dc20   91-27401
                                                            CIP

Typeset by Bookworks Plus
Color separation by United Sea Graphic Art Co., Ltd.
Printed and bound in Hong Kong by Leefung-Asco Printers Limited

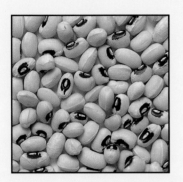

THE REDISCOVERED BEAN

Beans are inexpensive, versatile, packed with nutrition, easy to store, agriculturally enriching, delicious, and they are without a doubt one of the world's most valuable foods.

The edible seeds of a pod-bearing plant, dried or fresh beans and peas are nature's most balanced food. They are exceedingly low in fat and what fat they do contain is unsaturated. They are cholesterol-free yet help manage blood cholesterol and glucose, and they are high in vegetable protein, fiber, vitamins, and minerals.

Long thought of as peasant food, legumes are now afforded an honored spot in the culinary arts. Available in many sizes, shapes, colors, and flavors, they offer an almost limitless expansion to the cook's repertoire. Nearly every one of the world's cuisines has a superb dish featuring beans or peas. France's cassoulet, Louisiana's red beans and rice, Brazil's feijoada, Mexico's refried beans, the Middle East's hummus bi tahini, Cuba's black bean soup, Japan's red bean cake, and Italy's pasta e fagioli are but a few of the diverse and divine international recipes for legumes. With current interest in low-calorie, high-fiber diets and a commitment to good health, legumes are, once again, at the top of every good cook's list.

In this book, I have included old-fashioned and well-known recipes for Hoppin' John and simple cassoulet, which are often an integral part of a cook's repertoire. However, I think that the surprising gourmet turn given to the homey bean in such recipes as Bean Cakes with Caviar and Créme Fraîche and Grilled Red Snapper with Red Lentil Salsa places

© Steven Mark Needham/Envision

legumes in the center of the most innovative cooking today. Once you familiarize yourself with the general information about beans outlined in the Bean Index, (found on pages 12–13), all of the recipes in the book should be easy to accomplish.

Remember, all of the recipes included in this book are versatile, so that any dried legume can be used in place of any other one. If you don't like the flavor or texture of one type of bean, experiment using one of your favorites. Most recipes calling for meat or poul-

try as a main ingredient can be adjusted easily for a vegetarian diet by simple elimination or by replacing them with tofu or a hearty mushroom.

The brightest, most innovative chefs everywhere are reintroducing legumes into their restaurant menus. Their enthusiastic interest has sparked that of farmers who are rediscovering long lost or forgotten legumes; the snow cap, the appaloosa, tongues of fire, and the Christmas lima are but a few of these newfound beans. This lowly everyman's food is fast becoming an essential element in the new health-conscious cuisine. Wearing any number of its many disguises, the legume is a refined addition to the most polished dining table. Either combined with animal protein or working their vegetarian magic with rice, begin to introduce legumes into your daily diet. Remember, they are good enough to eat!

BUYING BEANS

It is very difficult to give exact guidelines for purchasing fine-quality dried legumes. I find it best to get them at the various ethnic shops where the turnover is heaviest, rather than at the supermarket. Following are suggestions on what to look for when buying legumes.

Fresh beans, peas, and sprouts should be crisp and free of any brown spots. If you are buying loose dried beans or peas, pick through them to eliminate dirt and pebbles and to ensure that you get them insect-free.

If legumes are packaged, make certain that the container is well sealed and, if possible, examine the contents by looking through any transparent part of the package. Due to absorption of moisture, one cup of dried beans or peas will produce approximately 2½ cups of cooked beans or peas.

Frozen beans and peas should be purchased only when the containers are clean, neat, and damage-free.

Canned beans, such as cannellini, kidney beans, and chick-peas, are often of excellent quality, and are exceedingly useful to keep on hand if they do not contain a glut of preservatives. Other beans and peas, such as green or lima beans or green peas, can be bought dried, canned, or frozen. However, there's absolutely no comparison to their fresh counterpart. I do not recommend their use.

© FPG International

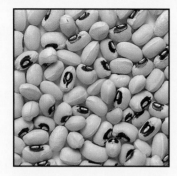

ADZUKI

The most basic bean of the Orient. Small, red-brown in color and extremely versatile.

Available fresh, sprouted, dried, or ground into a fine flour.

BLACK-EYED PEAS

Identified with the southern United States. Medium, pale yellow with a black heel (or dot). Thin skinned and quick cooking.

AKA Black-eyed beans, cow peas.

Available fresh, frozen, or dried.

CRANBERRY

Used most frequently in Italian cooking. Medium, pale pink with beige mottling. May be used interchangeably with pinto beans.

AKA Roman beans.

Available fresh, canned, or dried.

GREEN BEANS

Young, fresh, green edible pods of haricot beans. Also available as yellow wax beans or as the French *haricot vert* with little taste variation.

AKA Snap beans, string beans, haricots.

Available fresh, canned, and frozen.

BLACK BEANS

Native to South America. Small, with a shiny exterior and a rich interior.

AKA Turtle beans, *frijoles negros*.

Available dried.

CHICK-PEAS

Used extensively throughout the Mediterranean, India, and the Middle East. Round, medium, pale beige, and versatile.

AKA Garbanzos, *Ceci*.

Available dried, canned, sprouted, or ground into flour.

FAVA BEANS

Native to Europe and used throughout the Mediterranean. Large, clear, pale green when fresh; light brown and crenulated when dried. Fresh young pods are also edible.

AKA Broad bean, horse bean.

Available fresh, dried, or canned.

HARICOT BEANS

These are the many varieties of seeds of legumes. The mature seeds come in assorted sizes and may be either creamy white and slightly kidney shaped (Great Northern, navy, small white, white kidney, cannellini, and yankee beans), or pink to red to reddish brown kidney shapes (kidney red, pink, pinto, and Mexican beans). The immature seeds are known as flageolets and are the caviar of the bean world, removed from the pod when tender and just maturing.

Available dried.

LENTILS

Known as the biblical legume, lentils are probably the oldest cultivated legume.

Brown lentils, the most common variety, are small, soft, brown, quick-cooking discs.

Orange lentils, used most frequently in Middle Eastern or Indian cooking, are small, soft, orange discs.

AKA Egyptian lentils.

Green lentils are small, soft, olive-green discs and are known as the gourmet lentil. The best variety comes from the South of France.

Indian lentils are either red lentils in their seeds (brown masoor) or with the seed removed (masoor dal). All lentils are quick cooking.

Available dried.

LIMA BEANS

Native to Central and South America, with several varieties (forkhook, baby) now available. Fresh limas are a flat, pale-green pod holding either small pale-green seeds (baby limas) or large, almost white seeds.

AKA Butter beans.

Available fresh, frozen, canned, and dried.

MUNG BEANS

Native to India. A small, round bean whose primary use is as sprouts in Oriental cooking. May also be eaten whole.
Available dried, ground into flour, or sprouted.

PEAS

One of the oldest legumes, fresh green peas have been greatly coveted through the centuries for their delightful flavor. A recent variety of this ancient pleasure is the sugar snap pea, which can either be taken out of the pod or eaten in its entirety.

Snow peas, another green variety, are a staple of Oriental cooking.

Dried green or yellow split peas, the seeds of the succulent pod, are similar to the lentil in versatility and nourishment.

Available fresh, frozen, canned, or dried.

PIGEON PEAS

Native to Africa, these dried, round, beige peas are used throughout the Caribbean and the American South.

AKA *Gandules*, Congo beans.

Available canned and dried.

SOYBEANS

Native to China, these small, round, cream-colored beans are also known as the miracle bean. Used as a primary ingredient in a wide variety of products ranging from fuels to all manner of foodstuffs and, of course, as the number one bean of the Orient with its use as sauce, tofu, miso, tempeh, flour, and milk.

STORING BEANS

Fresh beans, peas, and sprouts must be refrigerated until used. Long storage is undesirable, and if refrigerated for a long period of time, they will rot.

Dried legumes are best stored in a cool spot in a see-through, airtight container. Do not store in damp, humid, or refrigerated conditions or the legumes will toughen. Dried legumes seem to keep indefinitely, but old ones may require a longer cooking time. Never freeze dried legumes.

Frozen and canned products should be stored as recommended on the individual package.

Freezing Cooked Beans

Bean soups and casseroles are perfect to make in advance and freeze for later use. Bean soups are, in fact, particularly good when they are given some extra time for the flavors to meld. When freezing, cover tightly and label with their name and the date frozen. Freeze for no more than one year.

COOKING WITH BEANS

Always soak dried beans in ten times as much water as beans, changing the water at least three times over a four-hour period. You can also allow beans to soak

© Sandy Roessler/FPG International

overnight if they are particularly old. However, on a long soak make certain that the beans are in a cool spot or they may begin to ferment. Discard all soaking liquids and refresh beans under cold running water before placing them in the cooking liquids you will be using. This will reduce the possibility of flatulence often associated with dried beans.

Flatulence is caused by the human body's inability to digest the bean's complex sugars, called oligosaccharides. Since they are not absorbed, these compounds are passed into the large intestine, where they become gaseous. Beans do not produce any more flatulence than that caused by other strongly flavored vegetables, nuts, or raisins. On the positive side, the gas formed by beans is more easily controlled than that produced by other foods. Presoaking will virtually eliminate the production of gases.

A healthy digestive system—one that gets plenty of fiber, leafy green vegetables, fruits, and legume protein—will have only a minimal problem absorbing oligosaccharides.

With the exception of lentils and split- and black-eyed peas, all dried beans and peas must be soaked before cooking to restore moisture and to reduce the power of the oligosaccharides. Before soaking, beans and peas should be picked clean of debris and well rinsed. I have described the best soaking method above.

Lentils, split peas, and black-eyed peas generally do not require any soaking. However, if you do choose to soak them they will cook in a matter of minutes. For firm cooked red lentils, soak them in very hot water to cover for 30 minutes, then place in rapidly boiling water for about 3 minutes. Drain well. Red lentils cook very fast and rapidly loose their intense color. If you follow these directions, the lentils will retain their color and shape for use in sauces or as a garnish.

Split- and black-eyed peas are generally cooked in liquid to cover for about 30 minutes. Fresh beans and peas are usually cooked in rapidly boiling salted water until tender and bright colored. As a rule, fresh green beans and peas require no more than 3 minutes, while other fresh seeds such as cranberry, fava, or lima beans will require additional cooking time. Watch them closely and be sure to never overcook tender, fresh beans and peas, as they will lose flavor and disintegrate.

When time does not allow a long soak, you can place clean, rinsed beans in a deep pot and cover with at least three inches of cool water. Cover the pot and place over high heat. Bring to a boil and boil for five minutes. Remove from the heat and allow to sit, covered, for no less than one hour and no more than two hours. Drain and rinse well before cooking.

After soaking, the drained, dried beans and peas should be placed in at least two inches of liquid to cover in a heavy-lidded saucepan. Bring to a boil over high heat. Immediately lower heat and gently simmer until tender, adding liquid as necessary.

Dried, soaked, drained legumes may be cooked in a pressure cooker or crockpot following the manufacturer's directions.

Microwave ovens are not suitable for cooking dried legumes.

Old Wives' Tales Disproved

❦ *Salt should* not *be added to bean-soaking water or to the cooking liquids until the beans are quite soft. Salt toughens the outer skin and will lessen the beans' absorption.*

❦ *Baking soda should* not *be used to soften dried legumes. It does, in fact, keep them from properly absorbing moisture and also destroys essential nutrients. However, if you must use hard water as a soaking or cooking liquid, add no more than ⅛ teaspoon of baking soda per cup of dried legumes to the water to facilitate moisture absorption.*

❦ *Acidic ingredients such as tomatoes or their juice, citrus, or pineapple should* not *be added when cooking dried legumes until they are quite soft. If added too early the acids will prevent them from softening.*

❦ *Dried legumes should never be boiled. A slow, gentle simmer produces the most digestible result.*

❦ *Cooked, dried legumes are easily pureed in a blender or food processor fitted with the metal blade, using a bit of the cooking liquid for thinning. If you do not have any remaining cooking liquid and the puree requires thinning, use vegetable, chicken, or beef stock or warm water, depending upon the other ingredients in the recipe.*

Note: An asterisk beside an ingredient indicates that the recipe for it is included elsewhere in the book.

CHAPTER ONE

APPETIZERS

WHITE BEAN PÂTÉ ❧ BLACK BEAN NACHOS

BEAN CAKES WITH CAVIAR AND CRÈME FRÂICHE

HUMMUS BI TAHINI ❧ CHICKEN CHUTNEY ❧ MIXED VEGETABLE PÂTÉ

INDIAN VEGETABLE FRITTERS WITH CURRY MAYONNAISE

SMOKED CHICKEN IN BLACK BEAN CREPES ❧ SOCCA

VEGETABLE PIE ❧ BEAN DIP

WHITE BEAN PÂTÉ

MAKES 1 8-INCH BY 4-INCH LOAF

1½	cups fresh bread crumbs
2	tablespoons canola oil
½	cup chopped shallots
3	cloves garlic, peeled and chopped
1	cup chicken stock (or beef or vegetable stock)
¼	cup grated carrots
¼	teaspoon ground cloves
1½	teaspoons minced fresh thyme
1	teaspoon minced fresh basil
2½	cups cooked, well-drained, dried white beans (see page 15)
2	large eggs
2	tablespoons dark beer
1	teaspoon fresh lime juice
¼	teaspoon Tabasco sauce (or to taste)
	Salt to taste
1½	cups cooked well-drained black beans
1	teaspoon minced fresh cilantro
½	teaspoon ground cumin
1	tablespoon melted unsalted butter or vegetable oil

Preheat oven to 375° F.

Grease an 8-inch by 4-inch loaf pan and generously coat it with ½ cup bread crumbs. Set aside.

Heat canola oil in heavy sauté pan over medium-high heat. When hot, add shallots and garlic and sauté for 4 minutes or until just soft. Add chicken stock, carrots, cloves, ½ teaspoon thyme, and basil and continue to cook for 5 minutes or until carrots are just soft. Remove from heat.

Place white beans in food processor fitted with the metal blade. Add chicken stock mixture and process until very smooth. When smooth, add eggs and beer. Process until well combined. Scrape bean puree into medium-sized mixing bowl. Stir in lime juice, Tabasco, remaining bread crumbs, and salt to taste. Taste and adjust seasoning if necessary.

Toss black beans with the remaining thyme, cilantro, cumin, and melted butter. Sprinkle one-third of this mixture over the bottom of the prepared pan. Fill one-half full with white bean puree and sprinkle top with additional one-third black beans. Cover with remaining white bean puree and smooth the top with a spatula. Press remaining black beans into the top and tightly seal entire pan with aluminum foil. Place in an ovenproof pan and pour in enough hot water to come halfway up the sides of the loaf pan. Place in a preheated oven and bake for 45 minutes or until a knife inserted into the center comes out dry. Remove from oven and place on wire rack. Place a weight on top of hot pâté and let stand at least 2 hours or until room temperature. Remove weight and refrigerate for 4 hours or until well chilled. When ready, unwrap and invert onto serving plate. (Dip pan in hot water for 1 minute to loosen pâté if necessary.) Serve with toast points and honey mustard or fruit chutney.

This pâté may be served hot, as a main course.

BLACK BEAN NACHOS
SERVES 6

12   6–inch blue corn tortillas

Approximately 1½ cups vegetable oil

½   cup chopped fresh tomatillos

¼   teaspoon minced fresh jalapeño pepper (or to taste)

½   cup chopped fresh tomatoes

¼   cup chopped red onions

1   clove garlic, peeled and chopped plus ½ teaspoon
    minced

2   tablespoons minced fresh cilantro

Salt to taste

Pepper to taste

1   tablespoon fresh lime juice

1½   cups cooked, well-drained, dried black beans (see
     page 15)

2   teaspoons bacon fat (or vegetable oil)

2   tablespoons minced onion

Tabasco to taste

¼   cup cooked crisp bacon (optional)

1   tablespoon diced red bell pepper

Approximately ½ cup sour cream

½   cup grated Monterey Jack or cheddar cheese

Approximately ½ cup chopped avocado

Using a 2-inch round biscuit cutter, cut circles from blue corn tortillas to make twenty-four 2-inch-round corn chips. Heat enough oil to measure ½ inch in a large cast-iron or other heavy skillet over high heat. When hot, fry the tortilla chips, a few at a time, turning once, for about 20 seconds or until crisp. Use tongs to immediately remove from oil and transfer to a paper towel to drain. Set aside. (You may substitute commercially prepared round blue corn chips.)

In a food processor fitted with the metal blade, coarsely chop the tomatillos, jalapeño pepper, tomato, red onion, garlic clove, and cilantro using quick on-and-off turns. Season with salt, pepper, and fresh lime juice and set aside to marinate.

Using a fork or potato masher, mash the black beans to make a chunky paste. Heat bacon fat or vegetable oil in a small, heavy skillet over medium heat. When hot, add mashed beans, onion, minced garlic, and Tabasco. Cook, stirring constantly, for 4 minutes or until beans are hot and well fried. Remove from heat and stir in bacon and red pepper until well combined. Set aside.

Preheat broiler.

Lay the tortilla chips out on a baking sheet. Coat each chip with a teaspoon of the black bean mixture. Top beans with tomatillo salsa and sprinkle with grated cheese. Place under a preheated broiler for about 15 seconds or until cheese has melted, but not browned. Remove from broiler. Place a dollop of sour cream in the center of each nacho and sprinkle with chopped avocado. Serve immediately.

BEAN CAKES WITH CAVIAR AND CRÈME FRAÎCHE

SERVES 6

3   cups cooked dried white or fava beans (see page 15)

3   cloves garlic, peeled

¼   cup chopped scallions

1   tablespoon chopped fresh cilantro

½   teaspoon ground cumin

½   teaspoon ground coriander

1   teaspoon baking powder

1   large egg yolk

    Salt to taste

    White pepper to taste

1   cup all-purpose flour

3   tablespoons canola oil (or other vegetable oil)

    Approximately ½ cup Crème Fraîche*

    Approximately ¼ cup golden caviar

Chop beans, garlic, scallions, cilantro, and spices in a food processor fitted with the metal blade, using quick on-and-off turns. Do not puree. Remove to a bowl and stir in baking powder, egg yolk, salt, and pepper. Cover and refrigerate for 1 hour.

When chilled, form into 12 2–inch patties and dredge in flour. Heat oil in large sauté pan over medium heat. When hot, add bean patties and sauté for 3 minutes per side or until golden brown. Remove from heat and drain on a paper towel. Keep warm.

Place patties on warm serving plates. Place a teaspoon of crème fraîche on top of each and sprinkle with golden caviar. Serve immediately.

CRÈME FRAÎCHE

MAKES 2 CUPS

2   cups heavy cream

4   tablespoons buttermilk

Combine heavy cream and buttermilk in a glass bowl or jar. Cover and allow to stand 24 hours at room temperature to thicken. When thick, refrigerate for 12 hours before use.

HUMMUS BI TAHINI

MAKES APPROXIMATELY 5 CUPS

1   pound dried chick-peas

6   cloves garlic, peeled and chopped

½   cup fresh lemon juice

1   cup tahini (sesame seed paste)

    Salt to taste

    White pepper to taste

¼   cup minced fresh parsley

Soak, rinse, and cook chick-peas. Drain, reserving liquid. Place the chick-peas, garlic, lemon juice, and tahini in a food processor fitted with the metal blade. Blend until smooth, adding reserved liquid as you go to make a thick puree. Season with salt and pepper. Scrape into serving bowl and sprinkle top with parsley. Serve with pita bread triangles as a scoop.

Any leftover hummus may be stored, covered, and refrigerated for up to one week.

Bean Cakes with Caviar and Crème Fraîche, accented with parsley.

CHICKEN CHUTNEY

SERVES 6

2	cups chopped cooked chicken breasts
¼	cup chopped scallions
1	tablespoon curry powder
½	cup mayonnaise
¾	cup mango chutney
¼	cup dried currants
½	cup cooked, well-drained, firm red lentils (see page 15)
1	tablespoon chopped fresh cilantro
6	cups chopped bitter salad greens (such as chicory, radicchio, endive)
2	tablespoons toasted coconut

Place chicken, scallions, curry powder, mayonnaise, and chutney in a food processor fitted with the metal blade. Chop, using quick on-and-off turns, until just combined. Do not puree. Place in a medium-sized mixing bowl and toss in currants, red lentils, and cilantro. Cover and refrigerate for 1 hour to allow flavors to blend.

Place a small mound of mixed greens on serving plates. Top with a mound of chicken chutney and sprinkle with toasted coconut. Serve immediately.

Chicken Chutney can also be served on individual leaves of endive, radicchio, or Boston lettuce, or on date-nut or pumpernickel bread triangles. Sprinkle the tops of each with toasted coconut.

MIXED VEGETABLE PÂTÉ

MAKES 1 8-INCH BY 4-INCH LOAF

10	large shiitake mushrooms
2	tablespoons olive oil
1	teaspoon grated orange zest
½	cup fresh orange juice
1	teaspoon minced garlic
2	tablespoons cognac
¼	cup unsalted butter or vegetable oil
1	pound carrots, peeled and chopped
¼	cup minced shallots
⅛	teaspoon freshly grated nutmeg
	Salt to taste
	White pepper to taste
1	teaspoon sugar
2	large eggs
2	tablespoons all-purpose flour
	Approximately 20 large, wilted, fresh spinach leaves
2½	cups cooked dried lima beans (see page 15)
1	cup cooked fresh peas
¼	teaspoon curry powder
¼	teaspoon grated fresh ginger
	Herb Butter*

Wipe mushrooms clean. Remove stems and set aside for another use.

Heat olive oil in medium-heavy sauté pan over medium heat. When hot, add mushrooms, stem side down. Sprinkle with orange zest, ¼ cup orange juice, and garlic. Cover and simmer for 4 minutes or until mushrooms begin to soften. Add cognac and raise heat to a boil. Boil for 3 minutes to allow alcohol to evaporate. Add remaining orange juice, lower heat, cover, and simmer for about 10 minutes or until mushrooms are quite soft and liquid has evaporated. Do not overcook. If liquid has not evaporated, raise heat and allow liquid to boil off. Remove mushrooms from pan and drain on a paper towel.

Melt butter in a medium-sized sauté pan over medium-high heat. Add carrots, shallots, nutmeg, and salt and pepper. Lower heat. Cover and cook, stirring frequently, for about 10 minutes or until carrots are beginning to soften. Remove cover, add sugar, and cook for an additional 3 minutes or until carrots are very soft. Scrape into food processor fitted with the metal blade and process until smooth. Add 1 egg and flour and process until well blended. Taste and adjust seasoning. Set aside.

Preheat oven to 375°F.

Grease an 8–inch by 4–inch loaf pan and line with slightly wilted, large spinach leaves, extending them over the sides to allow enough room to enclose the top. Set aside.

Place lima beans, peas, curry, ginger, 1 egg, and salt and pepper in food processor fitted with the metal blade. Process until smooth. Taste and adjust seasoning. Spoon into prepared pan and rap pan sharply to expel bubbles. Smooth top down. Layer drained mushrooms over top of bean puree to evenly coat. Spoon carrot puree on top of mushroom layer. Rap the pan again to expel bubbles. Smooth top and

enfold with spinach leaves. Cover top with a piece of oiled parchment or wax paper and tightly seal entire pan with aluminum foil.

Place in an ovenproof pan and pour in enough hot water to come halfway up the sides of loaf pan. Place in preheated oven and bake for about 90 minutes or until a knife inserted into the center comes out clean. Remove from oven and place on a wire rack. Remove foil and allow pâté to rest for 30 minutes. Place a serving platter over the top of the loaf pan and invert the pâté onto the platter. Cut into ½–inch slices and drizzle with Herb Butter. Serve immediately.

HERB BUTTER
MAKES 1 CUP

½   *cup unsalted butter*

½   *cup salted butter*

1   *tablespoon minced fresh tarragon*

1   *tablespoon minced fresh chervil*

1   *tablespoon minced fresh dill*

1   *teaspoon minced fresh basil*

Melt butter in the top half of a double boiler over hot water. Add herbs and allow to steep for at least 30 minutes. Keep warm until ready to serve.

INDIAN VEGETABLE FRITTERS WITH CURRY MAYONNAISE

MAKES APPROXIMATELY 3 CUPS OF VEGETABLES

1   cup chick-pea flour (available from East Indian or Middle Eastern markets and some specialty stores.)

⅛   teaspoon cayenne

½   teaspoon curry powder

¼   teaspoon ground cumin

½   teaspoon baking powder

    Salt to taste

    White pepper to taste

    Approximately ¾ cup warm water

    Approximately 4 cups vegetable oil

3   cups mixed fresh vegetable pieces (such as broccoli or cauliflower florets, onion rings, green beans, carrot slices, bell peppers, yams, or potato slices)

    Curry Mayonnaise*

Sift dry ingredients together in a medium-sized bowl. Whisk in enough warm water to make a loose batter. Cover and let stand for 1 hour.

Heat enough oil to measure at least 3 inches in a deep fryer. Bring to 350°F on a food thermometer. Whisk the batter and dip the vegetable pieces into it, one at a time, until well coated. Place battered vegetables into hot oil, a few at a time, and fry for 2 minutes or until golden, turning frequently. Transfer fried vegetables to a paper towel to drain. Keep warm until ready to serve, but do not cover. Serve warm with Curry Mayonnaise.

CURRY MAYONNAISE

MAKES ABOUT 1¾ CUPS OF MAYONNAISE

1½   cups mayonnaise

1   tablespoon curry powder

1   teaspoon ground cumin

1   tablespoon chopped fresh cilantro

1   tablespoon chopped scallion

1   teaspoon minced fresh green chili peppers (or to taste)

1   tablespoon orange blossom honey

1   teaspoon fresh lime juice

Place all ingredients in a blender and process until smooth. Serve cold.

Mixed Vegetable Pâté, perfect for company. See page 26.

SMOKED CHICKEN IN BLACK BEAN CREPES

SERVES 6

2 whole smoked chicken breasts (available through fine butchers or by mail order)

½ cup finely julienned jicama

¼ cup finely julienned red onions

1 cup sour cream

1 teaspoon ground cumin

1 teaspoon minced fresh mint

1 teaspoon minced fresh basil

 Salt to taste

 Pepper to taste

 Black Bean Crepes*

 Avocado Black Bean Sauce*

6 sprigs fresh cilantro

Skin and bone chicken breasts, if necessary. Slice diagonally into thin strips. Combine with jicama, red onions, sour cream, cumin, mint, basil, and salt and pepper.

Place about ¼ cup of the above filling into center of each warm Black Bean Crepe* and fold edges in to enclose filling. Turn over onto a serving plate, allowing 2 per person. Garnish with a cilantro sprig and serve immediately with Avocado Black Bean Sauce.*

BLACK BEAN CREPES

½ cup pureed, cooked, dried black beans (see page 15)

½ cup water

 Tabasco to taste

 Salt to taste

1 large egg

2 tablespoons melted unsalted butter

½ cup all-purpose flour

½ cup beer

Place beans, water, Tabasco, and salt in blender or food processor fitted with the metal blade. Cover and process until smooth. Add egg and butter and process until well blended. Add flour and beer and again process until a smooth, thin batter is reached. If too thick, add more water. Pour into an airtight container. Cover and refrigerate for 2 hours. Remove from refrigerator and test for consistency. You will want a thin, smooth batter that pours easily from a ladle. If it is too thick, stir in warm water, a bit at a time, until the desired consistency is reached.

Heat a 6-inch nonstick skillet or crepe pan over medium-high heat. When hot, rub with butter or vegetable oil and wipe clean. Pour about 2 tablespoons of batter into the center of the pan. Tilt the pan to make an even, thin layer of batter over the entire bottom. Return to heat and cook for about 1 minute or until edge is just browning. Lift the edge with a small spatula and turn crepe carefully over using a finger. Cook for another minute or until set. Remove to a piece of parchment paper or plastic wrap. Continue cooking until you have at least sixteen crepes (the extra will allow for any breakage when filling), placing wax paper between each crepe as you stack. Keep warm until ready to use. Crepes may be made several hours in advance if kept tightly wrapped. Rewarm in low oven or microwave.

AVOCADO BLACK BEAN SAUCE

2   ripe avocados

¾   cup sour cream

2   tablespoons chopped fresh cilantro

½   teaspoon chopped fresh mint

¼   teaspoon Tabasco (or to taste)

¼   cup fresh orange juice

1   teaspoon fresh lime juice
     Salt to taste

¼   cup finely diced red bell pepper

¼   cup finely diced green bell pepper

¼   cup cooked, well drained black beans (see page 15)

Peel and seed avocado. Place in food processor fitted with the metal blade and puree until smooth. Add sour cream, cilantro, mint, Tabasco, orange and lime juices, and salt and process until well blended. Scrape from processor bowl into a medium-sized mixing bowl. Stir in diced peppers and black beans. Taste and adjust seasoning. Cover and refrigerate if not using immediately.

SOCCA

MAKES 1 10-INCH TART

3   tablespoons extra virgin olive oil

1   cup hot water

½   teaspoon salt

2   tablespoons Herbes de Provence

1   cup chick-pea flour (available from East Indian or
     Middle Eastern markets and some specialty stores)

½   cup cooked chopped onions

Preheat oven to 350°F.

Coat a 10-inch tart pan with about 1 tablespoon olive oil. Combine hot water, salt, and 1 teaspoon Herbes de Provence. Then pour into flour, beating constantly. Pour into a medium-sized saucepan over medium heat and cook, stirring constantly, for 5 minutes. Spread into prepared tart pan. Brush with about 2 tablespoons olive oil and sprinkle with remaining Herbes de Provence and chopped onion.

Place in preheated oven and bake for 30 minutes or until golden and the surface has cracked. Remove from oven and cool on wire rack. Slice into wedges and serve immediately, or heat 3 tablespoons extra virgin olive oil in a heavy skillet over high heat. When hot, cut the socca into small pieces and fry a few at a time for about 1 minute until light brown. Drain on a paper towel and sprinkle with salt and pepper. Serve hot.

VEGETABLE PIE

MAKES 1 9-INCH PIE

2   cups all-purpose flour

½   teaspoon salt

¾   cup vegetable shortening

¼   cup ice water

2   cups cooked dried chick-peas (see page 15)

½   cup chopped onions

½   cup chopped carrots

½   cup chopped yams

½   cup chopped zucchini

½   cup chopped cabbage

½   cup chopped bell peppers

½   cup chopped parsnips

½   cup drained canned Italian plum tomatoes

3   tablespoons curry powder

2   teaspoons sesame seeds

1   teaspoon ground cumin

½   teaspoon ground turmeric

½   teaspoon dried mustard

¼   teaspoon ground coriander

      Dash Tabasco

      Salt to taste

      Pepper to taste

Mix flour and salt together in a bowl. Cut in shortening to resemble a coarse meal. Add water, a tablespoon at a time, to make a firm dough. Do not overmix. Divide into two equal portions. Wrap each in plastic wrap and refrigerate until ready to use.

Combine remaining ingredients. Allow to stand for 30 minutes. Taste and adjust seasoning.

Preheat oven to 500°F.

Remove dough from refrigerator and roll out each portion on a lightly floured board to make two circles about 11 inches in diameter. Place one circle in the bottom of a 9-inch pie plate, pressing to fit. Fill with vegetable mixture. Cover with remaining circle and pinch and crimp edges together, removing excess dough as you go.

Place in preheated oven and bake for 15 minutes. Lower heat to 375°F and bake for another 35 to 45 minutes or until crust is golden and vegetables are cooked. Remove from oven and let stand 15 minutes. Cut into wedges and serve hot with a dollop of sour cream, yogurt, or crème fraîche, if desired.

BEAN DIP

MAKES ABOUT 3½ CUPS

2   *tablespoons vegetable oil*

1   *tablespoon minced garlic*

¼   *cup chopped red onion*

1 to 2 jalapeño peppers, stemmed, seeded, and chopped (or to taste)

2   *cups pinto or red kidney bean puree*

2   *tablespoons chili powder*

½   *teaspoon chopped fresh oregano*

1   *cup grated Monterey Jack or white cheddar cheese*

Heat vegetable oil in large, heavy sauté pan over high heat. When hot, stir in garlic, onion, and jalapeño peppers. Lower heat and sauté for 3 minutes or until just soft. Add beans, chili powder, and oregano and cook, stirring constantly, for 5 minutes or until hot. Remove from heat and stir in cheese until melted. Keep warm over hot water until ready to serve. Serve warm with tortilla or pita chips.

CHAPTER TWO

SOUPS

LENTIL SOUP ❦ LENTIL-ONION SOUP WITH CHEDDAR CRUST

LENTIL SOUP WITH LAMB MEATBALLS ❦ PASTA E FAGIOLI

NAVY BEAN SOUP ❦ FLAGEOLET SOUP ❦ TUSCAN SOUP

PROVENÇAL BEAN SOUP ❦ MINESTRONE ❦ RED BEAN SOUP

SPLIT PEA SOUP ❦ FRESH PEA SOUP ❦ FRESH LIMA BEAN CHOWDER

POTAGE MONGOLE ❦ SHERRIED BLACK BEAN SOUP

LENTIL SOUP
SERVES 6

1 tablespoon vegetable oil

1 cup finely chopped onions

½ cup finely chopped carrots

½ cup finely chopped potatoes

½ cup finely chopped red bell peppers

1½ cups lentils, picked clean and rinsed

3 cups water

3 cups chicken, veal, or vegetable stock

2 teaspoons minced fresh dill

   Salt to taste

   Pepper to taste

½ cup cooked meat or poultry, cubed (meat is optional, but country ham, duck, or goose are particularly good in lentil soup)

Heat oil in a medium-sized sauté pan over high heat. When hot, add onions, carrots, potatoes, and red peppers. Lower heat and sauté for 3 minutes or until just soft. Remove from heat.

Pour lentils into deep saucepan. Add water and stock and scrape in vegetables. Add dill, salt, and pepper. Place over medium heat and cook, stirring frequently, for 45 minutes or until lentils are soft but not mushy. When done, remove from heat and stir in cooked meat or poultry, if desired. Serve hot.

LENTIL-ONION SOUP WITH CHEDDAR CRUST
SERVES 6 TO 8

2 pounds yellow onions

2 tablespoons olive oil

1 pound lentils, well rinsed

1 teaspoon minced garlic

1 tablespoon chopped fresh parsley

½ cup white wine

4 cups beef broth or vegetable stock

4 cups water

   Salt to taste

   Pepper to taste

   6 to 8 slices toasted French bread

1½ cups grated cheddar cheese

Peel and slice onions. Heat oil in heavy saucepan over high heat. When hot, add onions and stir to coat. Lower heat and sauté onions for about 10 minutes or until they begin to brown. Add lentils, garlic, parsley, white wine, beef broth or vegetable stock, and water. Raise heat and bring to a boil. When boiling, lower heat and simmer for about 1 hour until lentils are mushy. Add salt and pepper and continue to cook for 30 minutes.

Preheat oven to 400°F.

Pour equal portions of lentil soup into warm, oven-proof soup bowls. Lay a slice of toast on top of each and generously sprinkle with grated cheddar cheese. Place in preheated oven and bake for 3 minutes or until cheese has melted. Raise oven heat to broil. Place soup bowls under broiler for 30 seconds or until cheese is bubbly and golden. Serve immediately.

LENTIL SOUP WITH LAMB MEATBALLS
SERVES 6

1	*pound very lean ground lamb*
½	*cup minced onions*
1	*large egg*
½	*cup fine bread crumbs*
2	*tablespoons minced fresh mint*
1	*teaspoon minced fresh parsley*
¼	*teaspoon ground cumin*
	Salt to taste
	Pepper to taste
1	*recipe Lentil Soup**
1	*cup chopped fresh tomatoes*
2	*cups chopped fresh Swiss chard*
2	*bay leaves*
1	*teaspoon minced fresh thyme*
1	*teaspoon minced fresh sage*
	Grated zest of 1 lemon
1	*teaspoon fresh lemon juice*
2	*cups chicken stock*

Combine lamb, onions, egg, bread crumbs, mint, parsley, cumin, and salt and pepper. When well blended, form into small meatballs no larger than ½ inch in diameter. Cover and refrigerate for 1 hour.

Combine remaining ingredients in heavy stockpot over high heat. When soup comes to a boil, stir in chilled meatballs, a few at a time. When all meatballs have been added, lower heat and continue to cook for about 15 minutes or until meatballs are done. Discard bay leaves before serving. Serve hot.

PASTA E FAGIOLI

SERVES 6 TO 8

2   tablespoons olive oil

¾   cup chopped onions

½   cup chopped carrots

¼   cup chopped celery

3   cloves garlic, peeled and chopped

1½   cups diced pancetta, apple-smoked bacon, ham or
        smoked ham hocks, or a meaty ham bone (optional)

1   cup canned plum tomatoes with juice

3   cups fresh cranberry beans or cooked dried white or
        cannellini beans (see page 15)

1   teaspoon minced fresh sage

1   tablespoon minced fresh parsley

4   cups beef, chicken, or vegetable stock

     Salt to taste

     Pepper to taste

½   pound dried small tubular macaroni

¼   cup grated Parmesan cheese

2   tablespoons extra virgin olive oil

Heat oil in large stockpot over medium-high heat. When hot, stir in onions, carrots, celery, and garlic. Lower heat and sauté, stirring frequently, for about 7 minutes or until vegetables are soft. Do not brown. Add meat, if using, and continue to sauté for 5 minutes or until meat has browned.

Stir in tomatoes, beans, herbs, and stock. Raise heat and bring to a boil. When boiling, lower heat to a simmer and cook for about 1 hour, until beans are quite tender. (If using cooked, dried beans, cook for only about 30 minutes.) Remove 1 cup of beans and process in a food mill or food processor fitted with the metal blade. Then stir back into the soup. Add salt and pepper, then bring soup back to a boil over high heat. When boiling, stir in macaroni and cook for about 10 minutes or until pasta is al dente.

Ladle into warm soup bowls. Swirl Parmesan cheese into the top of each bowl and drizzle with extra virgin olive oil. Serve immediately.

NAVY BEAN SOUP

SERVES 6 TO 8

1   *pound dried navy beans*

1   *smoked ham bone*

1   *cup diced onions*

1½   *cups diced potatoes, skin on*

1   *cup diced carrots*

¼   *cup diced celery*

2   *cloves garlic, peeled and minced*

2   *tablespoons minced fresh parsley*

1   *teaspoon minced fresh thyme*

1   *bay leaf*

6   *cups water*

2   *cups vegetable, chicken, or beef stock*

1   *cup tomato puree*

    Salt to taste

    Pepper to taste

1   *cup heavy cream (optional)*

Prepare beans for cooking (see page 15). Place in stockpot with ham bone, onions, potatoes, carrots, celery, garlic, parsley, thyme, and bay leaf. Add the water and stock. Bring to a boil over high heat. Lower heat and simmer for about 2 hours or until beans are very soft, adding water as necessary. When beans are quite soft, stir in tomato puree and salt and pepper, and cook for an additional 30 minutes. Remove bay leaf and stir in cream. Serve immediately.

Variations:

    1. Add 2 cups diced ham when you add tomato puree.

    2. Replace ham bone with a chicken carcass.

    3. Add 1½ cups chopped kale.

    4. Add 2 cups chopped turnips.

FLAGEOLET SOUP
SERVES 6 TO 8

2   cups dried flageolets

½   cup chopped shallots

¼   cup chopped leeks, white part only

1   teaspon minced garlic, plus 16 cloves roasted

1   tablespoon minced fresh parsley

1   tablespoon minced fresh thyme

1   teaspoon minced fresh chervil

6   cups chicken or vegetable stock

     Approximately ½ cup heavy cream

     Salt to taste

     White pepper to taste

1   tablespoon chopped capers

Prepare beans for cooking (see page 15). Combine drained beans with shallots, leeks, minced garlic, parsley, thyme, chervil, and stock in a large, heavy saucepan over medium-high heat. Bring to a boil. When boiling, lower heat and simmer for 1½ hours or until beans are tender. Remove from heat.

Squeeze roasted garlic cloves from skin and stir into soup. Place soup in food processor fitted with the metal blade and puree until smooth. Return to saucepan and stir in enough heavy cream to make a medium-thick soup. Add salt and pepper.

Return to medium heat and cook until just heated through. Serve hot, garnished with chopped capers.

TUSCAN SOUP
SERVES 6 TO 8

¼   cup extra virgin olive oil

1½   cups chopped red onions

1   tablespoon minced fresh rosemary

2   tablespoons minced fresh Italian parsley

½   teaspoon red pepper flakes (or to taste)

1   cup chopped, drained, canned Italian plum tomatoes

1½   pounds escarole or red cabbage, shredded

1   cup sliced carrots

5   cups vegetable broth

3   cups cooked dried white, cannellini, or navy beans (see page 15)

     Salt to taste

     Pepper to taste

Heat oil in heavy saucepan over medium heat. When hot, add onions and sauté, stirring frequently for 10 minutes or until onions begin to turn light brown. Stir in rosemary, parsley, red pepper flakes, and tomatoes and cook for 10 minutes. Stir in cabbage and cook for about 5 minutes or until cabbage has wilted. Add carrots, vegetable broth, and beans with salt and pepper and cook for 30 minutes. Serve hot with slices of crusty Italian bread brushed with olive oil, minced garlic, and minced fresh parsley and then lightly toasted.

Savory Tuscan Soup, served with crusty Italian bread.

PROVENÇAL BEAN SOUP
SERVES 6 TO 8

3   *tablespoons extra virgin olive oil*

1   *cup chopped red onions*

2   *cups chopped, cored, and peeled fresh tomatoes*

2   *teaspoons Herbes de Provence*

1   *tablespoon minced fresh parsley*

2   *cups cooked cranberry, appaloosa, tongues of fire, or other red beans (fresh or dried)*

2   *cups cooked fava beans (fresh or dried)*

1   *cup dry white wine*

2   *large pieces fresh orange peel, pith removed*

1   *cup diced carrots*

1   *cup diced zucchini*

1   *cup diced potatoes*

     Salt to taste

     Pepper to taste

     Pesto*

½   *cup grated Parmesan cheese*

Heat olive oil in a large, heavy saucepan over medium-high heat. When hot, add onions and sauté for about 5 minutes or until soft and beginning to brown. Stir in tomatoes, Herbes de Provence, and parsley and cook for 10 minutes. Raise heat and add cooked beans, wine, orange peel, and enough water to cover by 2 inches. Bring to a boil, then lower heat and stir in carrots, zucchini, potatoes, and salt and pepper. Cook for about 30 minutes or until vegetables are soft and the soup is well balanced in flavor.

Pour into hot soup bowls and stir in 1 teaspoon of Pesto* or to taste. Sprinkle with grated Parmesan cheese and serve immediately.

PESTO
MAKES APPROXIMATELY 2 CUPS

2   *cups fresh parsley*

2   *cups fresh basil leaves*

4   *cloves garlic, peeled and chopped*

½   *cup pine nuts or walnuts*

     Approximately ¾ cup extra virgin olive oil

¾   *cup grated Parmesan cheese*

     Salt to taste

Place parsley, basil, garlic, and pine nuts in food processor fitted with the metal blade. Process, using quick on-and-off turns, until well combined. With the motor running, slowly add olive oil until a smooth paste forms. Add the cheese and process to combine. Taste and add salt if necessary. Scrape into container, cover, and set aside until ready to use. Refrigerate if necessary.

MINESTRONE

SERVES 6 TO 8

¼   *cup extra virgin olive oil or vegetable oil*

¼   *cup unsalted butter or margarine*

1   *cup chopped onions*

1   *cup chopped leeks*

¼   *cup minced fresh Italian parsley*

2   *cups diced potatoes*

2   *cups diced carrots*

1   *cup diced celery*

1   *cup diced zucchini*

1   *cup diced yellow squash*

1   *cup chopped green or yellow wax beans*

1   *cup fresh (or frozen) green peas*

½   *cup diced parsnips or turnips*

1   *cup chopped Savoy cabbage*

2   *cups canned Italian plum tomatoes with juice*

6   *cups chicken, beef, or vegetable stock*

1   *large piece very dry crust from fresh Parmesan cheese (optional) plus ¼ cup grated*

2   *cups cooked dried cannellini or Great Northern beans (see page 15)*

Salt to taste

Pepper to taste

Heat oil and butter in a large stockpot over medium-high heat. When hot, stir in onions, leeks, and parsley. Lower heat and sauté for about 5 minutes or until onions are golden. Add remaining vegetables, one at a time, sautéing each for about 3 minutes. When all vegetables are sautéd, stir in tomatoes and stock. Raise heat and bring to a boil. When boiling, lower heat to a simmer. Add optional cheese crust and cook, stirring frequently, for at least 2 hours or until soup is very thick. Add cooked, dried beans and salt and pepper and cook for an additional 15 minutes. Remove cheese crust and ladle soup into hot bowls. Sprinkle with grated Parmesan cheese and serve immediately.

Variations:

1. You may replace any vegetable in this soup with any other you desire.

2. Cooked rice or pasta may be added when you add the beans and 1¼ teaspoon of Pesto* per serving may be swirled in just before serving.

3. Fresh beans, such as fava, cranberry, or white beans, may be used in place of cooked dried beans. If so, sauté along with other vegetables.

RED BEAN SOUP

SERVES 6 TO 8

1   *pound dried red beans*

2   *tablespoons canola oil*

1   *cup chopped red onions*

½   *cup chopped carrots*

¼   *cup chopped celery*

2   *tablespoons minced fresh parsley*

3   *cups chicken stock*

1   *cup roasted red peppers*

½   *teaspoon minced fresh marjoram*

½   *teaspoon minced fresh dill*

     Salt to taste

     Pepper to taste

1½   *cups heavy cream*

     Juice of 1 lime

½   *cup chopped hard-boiled egg (optional)*

1   *tablespoon chopped fresh Italian parsley (optional)*

Soak, rinse, and cook beans (see page 15). When cooked, drain off and reserve liquid. Divide beans into 2 equal portions and set aside.

Heat oil in large saucepan over high heat. When hot, add onions, carrots, celery, and parsley. Lower heat and sauté for 3 minutes or until vegetables start to soften. Stir in chicken stock, roasted peppers, marjoram, dill, and salt and pepper. Continue to cook for 10 minutes or until liquid is reduced by half. Scrape into food processor fitted with the metal blade. Add half of the beans and process until smooth. Add heavy cream and process until well incorporated. Add reserved bean cooking liquid if soup is too thick. Return to saucepan and add remaining beans. Taste and adjust seasoning.

Return to medium heat and cook until heated through. Stir in lime juice and pour into warm soup bowls. Sprinkle with chopped egg and parsley, if desired.

This soup may be served cold. However, if doing so, puree all beans.

SPLIT PEA SOUP

SERVES 6 TO 8

1   *pound green or yellow split peas*

1   *large ham bone*

2   *medium carrots, peeled and chopped*

1   *large, sweet onion stuck with 3 cloves*

1   *stalk celery, washed and chopped*

2   *tablespoons plus 2 teaspoons chopped fresh dill*

3   *quarts water or chicken or vegetable stock*

     Salt to taste

     Tabasco to taste

1   *teaspoon fresh lemon juice*

1   *cup freshly toasted rye bread croutons*

Wash and drain peas. Place in a heavy stockpot with ham bone, carrots, onion, celery, and 1 tablespoon dill. Add water or stock and bring to a boil over high heat. When boiling, lower heat to a simmer. Cover and simmer for about 1 hour or until peas are soft and soup is thickened. Remove from heat and discard the ham bone and onion. Stir in salt, Tabasco, and lemon juice. (If desired, puree in a food processor fitted with the metal blade and thin with heavy cream and chicken or vegetable stock.) Serve hot, garnished with croutons and remaining chopped fresh dill.

Variations:

1. Use any herb or spice you desire. For instance, 2 teaspoons curry powder is a great addition.

2. Eliminate the ham bone and use vegetable stock as the cooking liquid: puree, chill, and then stir in 1 tablespoon chopped fresh mint and 1 cup sour cream.

3. As a hearty meal: Before serving stir in 1 pound cooked sausage, diced ham, or any other smoked meat or poultry.

FRESH PEA SOUP

SERVES 6 TO 8

2	tablespoons unsalted butter
2	cups chopped Boston lettuce
6	cups shelled fresh peas (thawed frozen may be substituted)
1	cup chopped scallions
½	cup chopped fresh mint (or to taste)
4	cups chicken stock
	Salt to taste
	White pepper to taste
1	cup heavy cream
1	tablespoon fresh lemon juice (or to taste)
2	tablespoons sour cream or crème fraîche

Coat bottom and sides of medium-heavy saucepan with butter. Lay lettuce on bottom. Combine peas and scallions and 2 tablespoons chopped mint and add to saucepan. Pour in 1 cup chicken stock, cover, and place over medium-low heat for 5 minutes or until lettuce has wilted and exuded its moisture and peas begin to soften. Add remaining stock and salt and pepper. Raise heat and bring to a boil.

When boiling, lower heat and simmer for 20 minutes or until liquid has reduced by about one third. Remove from heat and pour into food processor fitted with the metal blade. Process until very smooth. Return to saucepan and stir in heavy cream. Place over medium heat and cook until just heated through. Whisk in lemon juice, taste, and adjust seasonings. Pour into warm serving bowls and place a dollop of sour cream or crème fraîche in the center and garnish with remaining chopped mint.

This soup may also be served cold.

© Steven Mark Needham/Envision

FRESH LIMA BEAN CHOWDER
SERVES 6 TO 8

3 *tablespoons butter or vegetable oil*

1 *cup chopped leeks, white part only*

3 *cloves garlic, peeled and chopped*

6 *cups fresh lima beans*

1 *teaspoon minced fresh jalapeño pepper (or to taste)*

2 *tablespoons minced fresh cilantro*

6 *cups chicken stock*

2 *cups cooked baby lima beans (see page 15)*

2 *cups cooked fresh corn*

½ *cup diced red bell peppers*

½ *cup diced green bell peppers*

½ *cup diced red onions*

1 *tablespoon fresh lime juice*

   Tabasco to taste

   Salt to taste

Heat butter in a medium-sized saucepan over medium heat. When hot, add leeks and garlic and sauté for 3 minutes or until beginning to soften. Stir in fresh lima beans, jalapeño pepper, 2 teaspoons cilantro, and chicken stock. Bring to a boil.

When boiling, lower heat and simmer for 30 minutes or until beans are soft. Remove from heat and puree in food processor fitted with the metal blade. Thin, if necessary, with hot chicken stock or heavy cream. Return to saucepan and stir in cooked baby lima beans, corn, red and green bell peppers, and red onions. Place over medium heat and cook for 5 minutes or until soup is very hot.

Remove from heat and stir in remaining cilantro, lime juice, Tabasco, and salt. Serve immediately.

Fresh Lima Bean Chowder, delicious with crackers.

© Peter Johansky

POTAGE MONGOLE
SERVES 6 TO 8

3   tablespoons butter

½   cup chopped onions

½   cup chopped shallots

1   tablespoon curry powder

½   teaspoon ground coriander

       Cayenne to taste

4   cups chicken stock

2   cups cooked, drained split peas (see page 15)

1½   cups fresh tomato puree

¼   cup finely julienned carrots

¼   cup finely julienned celery

¼   cup finely julienned red bell peppers

       Approximately 1 cup heavy cream

1   tablespoon fresh lime juice

       Salt to taste

       White pepper to taste

1   cup cooked wild rice (optional)

1   cup finely julienned breast of chicken

¼   cup diced fresh seedless tomatoes

2   tablespoons minced fresh parsley

Heat butter in heavy saucepan over medium heat. When hot, add onions and shallots and sauté for 5 minutes or until soft. Stir in curry powder, coriander, and cayenne. When well blended, add chicken stock, split peas, and tomato puree. Cook, stirring frequently, for about 30 minutes or until mixture is quite thick.

While soup is cooking, quickly blanch julienned vegetables, one at a time, in boiling, salted water. Refresh under cold running water, drain, and set aside.

When soup is done puree in food processor fitted with the metal blade. Strain soup back into saucepan, and whisk in heavy cream, ¼ cup at a time, lime juice, and salt and pepper. Do not allow soup to get too thin. Place over medium heat and stir in julienned vegetables and optional rice and/or chicken. Cook without stirring until just hot. Pour into warm soup bowls and garnish with diced tomatoes and parsley.

© Steven Mark Needham/Envision

SHERRIED BLACK BEAN SOUP
SERVES 6 TO 8

1½   cups dried black beans

2   medium carrots, peeled and chopped

1   cup peeled and chopped fresh pumpkin or hard squash (optional)

1   cup chopped celery, leaves included

1   cup chopped onions

2   cloves garlic, peeled

2   tablespoons minced fresh parsley

1   small smoked ham bone (optional)

8   cups cold water

½   pound pancetta or salt pork (optional)

1   tablespoon ground cumin

½   teaspoon minced fresh thyme

1   tablespoon fresh lemon juice

   Salt to taste

   Pepper to taste

½   cup dry sherry

½   cup finely chopped or sieved hard-boiled egg white

6   very thin lemon slices

Prepare beans for cooking (see page 15). Place beans, carrots, pumpkin, celery, onions, garlic, parsley, smoked ham bone, and cold water in a stockpot over high heat. Bring to a boil. Lower heat and simmer for about 2 hours or until beans are very soft.

While beans are cooking, cut pancetta (or salt pork) into ½-inch cubes, if using. Place in a small sauté pan over medium heat and fry, turning frequently, for about 15 minutes or until fat is rendered out and cubes are lightly browned. Discard fat and drain cubes on a paper towel. Set aside.

When beans are mushy, remove ham bone and discard. Stir in cumin, thyme, lemon juice, and salt and pepper. Continue to cook over low heat for 30 minutes. Remove from heat and puree in batches, if desired, in a food processor fitted with the metal blade.

When soup is pureed, return to stockpot and stir in sherry and reserved crispy pancetta cubes. Taste and adjust seasoning. Return to low heat and cook for about 5 minutes or until heated through.

Remove from heat and pour into hot soup bowls. Garnish top with egg white and a lemon slice. Serve immediately.

CHAPTER THREE

SALADS

HARICOT VERT, ORANGE, RED ONION SALAD

SCALLOP AND GREEN LENTIL SALAD ❧ WARM PORK AND LENTIL SALAD

TUSCAN SUMMER SALAD ❧ LENTIL SALAD ❧ GERMAN YELLOW BEAN SALAD

RUSSIAN BEAN SALAD ❧ SUMMER SEAFOOD AND BEAN SALAD

SALAD NIÇOISE ❧ GREEK POTATO SALAD

SOUTHWESTERN CHICKEN SALAD ❧ CARIBBEAN SHRIMP SALAD

PICKLED BEAN SALAD

HARICOT VERT, ORANGE, AND RED ONION SALAD

SERVES 6 TO 8

1½   *pounds haricots verts or very small fresh green beans*

4   *oranges (use blood oranges if available)*

1   *large red onion*

1¼   *cups canola oil*

½   *cup balsamic vinegar*

½   *cup grainy mustard*

2   *tablespoons fresh orange juice*

1   *teaspoon pure maple syrup*

1   *tablespoon chopped fresh mint*

   Salt to taste

   White pepper to taste

1   *large head red-leaf lettuce*

¼   *cup chopped, toasted pecans*

Wash and trim haricots verts. Place in top half of steamer over boiling water and steam for 2 minutes or until crisp and tender. Do not overcook.

Remove from steamer and quickly shock under cold running water. When well chilled, place on a paper towel to drain.

Peel and remove any pith from oranges. Slice crosswise into very thin slices. Set aside.

Peel and trim onion. Slice crosswise into very thin slices. Set aside.

Combine oil, vinegar, mustard, orange juice, maple syrup, mint, and salt and pepper in food processor fitted with the metal blade; process for 30 seconds or until well combined. Taste and adjust seasonings.

Wash and dry lettuce leaves and place on a serving plate. Place a circle of alternate slices of orange and red onion about 1 inch from the rim with edges slightly overlapping. Toss haricots verts with half of the dressing and place in the middle of the platter. Drizzle remaining dressing over the oranges, red onions, and lettuce leaves. Sprinkle with pecans and serve immediately.

Colorful Haricot Vert, Orange, and Red Onion Salad.

SCALLOP AND GREEN LENTIL SALAD
SERVES 6 TO 8

1   pound French green lentils

     Peel from one large orange, plus 1 teaspoon grated
       rind

2   cups dry white wine

4   cups cold water

¾   cup fresh orange juice

2   tablespoons sherry wine vinegar

½   cup extra virgin olive oil

4   cloves garlic, roasted and peeled

1   tablespoon Dijon mustard

     Salt to taste

     Pepper to taste

¼   cup cognac

¼   cup unsalted butter

     24 to 36 scallops, well trimmed

8   cups chopped watercress

½   cup toasted, chopped black walnuts (or any nut you
       prefer)

Bring lentils, orange peel, white wine, and water to a boil in a heavy saucepan over high heat. Lower heat to a simmer and cook for about 30 minutes or until lentils are just tender. When tender, drain off all liquid and discard orange peel.

While lentils are still warm, place in a bowl and stir in ¼ cup orange juice, vinegar, olive oil, roasted garlic, mustard, and salt and pepper. Taste and adjust seasonings. Cover and set aside to marinate.

Place remaining orange juice, cognac, butter, and grated orange rind in a heavy sauté pan over medium heat. Cook, stirring constantly, for about 5 minutes or until reduced by half. Add scallops and sauté for about 4 minutes, turning frequently, or until scallops are just warmed through. Remove from pan and keep warm.

Place a mound of lentils in the center of serving plates. Surround the lentils with watercress and lay four scallops on the greens at the "twelve," "three," "six," and "nine" o'clock positions. Drizzle any pan juices over the scallops and sprinkle with toasted walnuts. Serve immediately.

WARM PORK AND LENTIL SALAD
SERVES 6 TO 8

1   2-pound pork tenderloin, well trimmed of fat

1   teaspoon cayenne

2   tablespoons fresh lemon juice

2   tablespoons light soy sauce

4   cups cooked, drained, firm red lentils (see page 15)

½   pound fresh goat cheese, crumbled

2   tablespoons minced shallots

3   tablespoons minced fresh Italian parsley

3   tablespoons peanut oil

1   teaspoon Dijon mustard

1   teaspoon minced fresh thyme

     Salt to taste

     Pepper to taste

4   cups chicory, trimmed, washed, and dried

Preheat oven to 500°F.

Rub tenderloin with cayenne, 1 tablespoon lemon juice, and soy sauce. Place on rack in roasting pan. Place in preheated oven and roast for 15 minutes. Lower heat to 375°F and cook for an additional 30 minutes or until center is cooked. Remove from oven and keep warm. Lower oven to 300°F.

Combine lentils, goat cheese, shallots, 1 tablespoon parsley, remaining lemon juice, oil, mustard, thyme, and salt and pepper. Set aside.

Cover ovenproof platter with chicory. Slice pork tenderloin and, holding slices together, place them down the center of the platter on the chicory. Place equal portions of the lentil mixture on either side of the pork and return to 300°F oven for 5 minutes. Remove from oven, sprinkle with remaining parsley, and serve immediately.

TUSCAN SUMMER SALAD
SERVES 6 TO 8

2	*pounds grilled or roasted chicken breasts, cubed*
2	*cups cooked, drained, fresh fava beans (see page 15)*
1	*cup diced red onions*
½	*cup diced red bell peppers*
½	*cup diced celery*
¼	*cup minced fresh Italian parsley*
½	*cup extra virgin olive oil*
2	*tablespoons red wine vinegar*
3	*cloves garlic, roasted and peeled*
1	*teaspoon minced fresh thyme*
	Salt to taste
	Pepper to taste
2	*heads radicchio*
¼	*pound thinly sliced pecarino cheese*
	Coarsely ground pepper to taste

Combine all ingredients except radicchio, cheese, and coarsely ground pepper. Cover and allow to marinate for about 1 hour.

Wash and thoroughly dry the radicchio. Slice into a fine julienne. Place chicken salad in the center of a serving plate. Sprinkle with radicchio and thinly sliced pecarino. Sprinkle on coarsely ground pepper.

Serve immediately.

LENTIL SALAD

SERVES 6 TO 8

2	cups cooked, drained, warm lentils (see page 15)
1	cup diced red onions
2	cups diced skinless, seeded very ripe tomatoes
¼	cup chopped fresh parsley
2	tablespoons chopped fresh mint
¼	cup olive oil
4	tablespoons balsamic vinegar
1	teaspoon grainy mustard
	Salt to taste
	Pepper to taste

Combine all ingredients and allow to marinate for 1 hour at room temperature before serving. Serve at room temperature as is or on a bed of leaf lettuce.

Variations:

1. Add 1 cup diced, fried pancetta or 1 cup chopped, cooked bitter greens.
2. Add 2 cups sliced, cooked new potatoes.

GERMAN YELLOW BEAN SALAD

SERVES 6 TO 8

1½	pounds yellow wax beans, washed and well trimmed
½	pound lean bacon
1	cup diced sweet onions
¼	cup white wine vinegar
1	teaspoon caraway seeds
¼	cup chopped scallions
1	teaspoon chopped sweet pickle
	Salt to taste
	White pepper to taste

Bring 3 quarts of water to boil in a heavy saucepan over high heat. When boiling, add beans. Lower heat and simmer for about 3 minutes or until just tender. Drain and keep warm.

Fry bacon in a heavy skillet over medium-low heat for about 10 minutes or until crisp. Remove bacon to a paper towel to drain, but leave skillet on the heat.

Place diced onions in bacon fat. Raise heat to medium-high and cook, stirring frequently, for about 5 minutes or until onion begins to brown. Stir in vinegar, caraway seeds, and scallions and cook for 2 minutes. Stir in pickle and salt and pepper and pour over warm green beans. Toss to coat. Taste and adjust seasonings. Crumble bacon and sprinkle over the top. Serve immediately.

You may turn this into a main-course salad by adding quartered, cooked new potatoes and sliced, cooked knockwurst.

German Yellow Bean Salad, here served with knockwurst and new potatoes.

RUSSIAN BEAN SALAD

SERVES 6 TO 8

⅓ cup sour plum preserves (any plum preserves may be substituted)

2 tablespoons cider vinegar

½ cup sour cream

3 cups cooked, drained, dried red kidney beans (see page 15)

½ cup chopped fresh parsley

½ cup chopped fresh cilantro

1 tablespoon minced garlic

¼ cup chopped scallions

   Salt to taste

   Pepper to taste

Heat the preserves and vinegar in a small saucepan over medium heat. Cook, stirring constantly, for 3 minutes or until preserves have melted. Remove from heat and pour into a blender. Add sour cream and process until smooth.

Combine sour cream mixture with remaining ingredients. Cover and allow to marinate for at least 3 hours. Serve at room temperature.

SUMMER SEAFOOD AND BEAN SALAD

SERVES 6 TO 8

2 cups cooked, drained, dried beans of your choice (see page 15)

2 cups cooked, drained fresh green peas

2 cups cooked, drained haricot vert

½ cup chopped scallions

¼ cup minced fresh parsley

2 tablespoons chopped capers

1 tablespoon minced cornichon or other sour pickle

2 cups mayonnaise

   Juice of 1 lemon

2 pounds cooked, mixed seafood (such as shrimp, squid, lobster, tuna, eel)

3 very ripe tomatoes, peeled, cored, and quartered

Combine beans, peas, haricot verts, scallions, parsley, capers, and cornichon. When well combined, stir in 1 cup mayonnaise and half of the lemon juice. Combine remaining mayonnaise and lemon juice with the cooked seafood and place in the center of a serving platter. Surround the seafood with beans and garnish the edge of the platter with tomato quarters. Serve immediately.

Russian Bean Salad, accented with parsley and garlic.

SALAD NIÇOISE
SERVES 6 TO 8

1½   pounds fresh tuna steak, about ½ inch thick

¾   cup extra virgin olive oil

1   tablespoon fresh lemon juice

     Salt to taste

     Pepper to taste

2   cups cooked, sliced new potatoes

2   cups cooked, drained, dried white beans (cannellini or
     any other white bean will do) (see page 15)

1   large red onion, peeled and sliced into rings

1   tablespoon chopped capers

2   tablespoons chopped fresh Italian parsley

1   tablespoon chopped fresh basil

2   tablespoons balsamic vinegar

2   tablespoons white wine vinegar

1   tablespoon Dijon mustard

1   large head red-leaf lettuce, washed and dried

2   cups diced ripe tomatoes

4   hard-boiled eggs, quartered

6   cooked artichoke hearts, quartered

¼   cup drained anchovy fillets

¼   cup Niçoise olives

Coat tuna steak with 2 tablespoons olive oil and lemon juice and season with salt and pepper. Prepare grill or preheat broiler. Grill tuna, turning once, for about 6 minutes or until just cooked. Remove from grill and set aside.

Combine potatoes, beans, onions, capers, parsley, basil, remaining oil, vinegars, mustard, and salt and pepper. Break the tuna into bite-size chunks and toss into potato mixture.

Line a large serving platter with red-leaf lettuce. Mound the tuna mixture in the center. Place tomatoes in a circle around the tuna salad. Garnish plate with quartered hard-boiled eggs, artichoke hearts, anchovies, and Niçoise olives. Serve immediately.

GREEK POTATO SALAD
SERVES 6 TO 8

1½   cups Greek olive oil

½   cup fresh lemon juice

10   anchovy fillets

½   teaspoon minced fresh oregano

1   tablespoon minced fresh parsley

2   tablespoons yogurt

1   clove garlic, peeled

1   large hard-boiled egg

     Salt to taste

     Pepper to taste

1½   pounds new potatoes

2   cups cooked, well-drained, dried chick-peas (page 15)

½   pound feta cheese, crumbled

¼   cup pitted Calamata olives

½   cup diced red onions

1   cup cored, seeded, and diced ripe tomatoes

Process olive oil, lemon juice, anchovy fillets, oregano, parsley, yogurt, garlic, egg, and salt and pepper in a blender until well combined. Set aside.

Wash and quarter potatoes and place in a medium-sized saucepan. Cover with water and bring to a boil over high heat. Lower heat and simmer for about 10 minutes or until tender. Drain well. Place in a salad bowl and pour half of the vinaigrette over warm potatoes. Toss to combine. Set aside to cool at room temperature.

When cool, toss in remaining ingredients. Stir in remaining vinaigrette and serve at room temperature. Garnish with additional anchovy fillets, if desired.

SOUTHWESTERN CHICKEN SALAD

SERVES 6 TO 8

4	*cups cubed, cooked chicken breast*
2	*cups cooked, drained, dried black beans (see page 15)*
¾	*cup diced red onions*
¼	*cup diced red bell peppers*
¼	*cup diced yellow bell peppers*
¼	*cup diced green bell peppers*
½	*cup diced jicama*
¼	*cup chopped fresh cilantro*
½	*cup mayonnaise*
¼	*cup sour cream*
2	*cloves garlic, roasted and peeled*
1	*teaspoon minced jalapeño pepper (or to taste)*
1	*teaspoon fresh lime juice*
	Salt to taste
	Pepper to taste
1	*cup toasted pine nuts*

Combine chicken, black beans, onions, bell peppers, jicama, and cilantro in a large bowl. Set aside. Whisk mayonnaise and sour cream together. When well blended, stir in garlic, jalapeño pepper, and lime juice. When combined, add to chicken and toss to blend. Stir in salt and pepper. Refrigerate for at least 30 minutes before serving to allow flavors to blend. Just before serving, add penne if using, toss in pine nuts. Serve as is or on a bed of lettuce.

CARIBBEAN SHRIMP SALAD
SERVES 6

1	large head leaf lettuce or any other curly-edged lettuce
1½	cups cooked, cleaned, and deveined medium shrimp
2	cups cooked (dried or fresh) black-eyed peas (page 15)
2	cups cooked rice
½	cup diced green bell pepper
½	cup diced red onions
⅓	cup peanut oil
½	cup fresh lime juice
¼	cup chopped fresh parsley or cilantro
1	teaspoon hot pepper sauce
	Salt to taste
	Pepper to taste
2	ripe avocados, peeled, seeded, and sliced
2	ripe papayas, peeled, seeded, and sliced
1	cup chopped, roasted, unsalted peanuts

Pull lettuce apart. Wash and dry leaves well. Generously line a serving platter with leaves. Refrigerate.

Combine shrimp, peas, rice, bell pepper, red onions, oil, ¼ cup fresh lime juice, parsley or cilantro, hot pepper sauce, and salt and pepper. Stir until well combined. Cover and refrigerate for about 1 hour.

Remove lettuce-lined platter and shrimp salad from refrigerator. Using a slotted spoon, carefully place shrimp salad in the center of lettuce. Place alternate slices of avocado and papaya around the edge of the shrimp salad. Sprinkle on any remaining dressing and the remaining lime juice. Garnish with chopped peanuts and serve immediately.

PICKLED BEAN SALAD
SERVES 6 TO 8

1	cup red wine vinegar
¼	cup light brown sugar
½	teaspoon salt (or to taste)
1	tablespoon minced garlic
1	dried pasilla chili pepper
4	cups cooked, drained, dried black beans (see page 15)
2	cups cooked pearl onions
1	red hot chili pepper, seeded and julienned (or to taste)
1	cup diced cooked ham
½	cup diced green bell peppers
3	hard-boiled eggs, peeled and quartered (optional)
¼	cup chopped black olives (optional)

Combine vinegar, brown sugar, salt, garlic, and pasilla chili pepper in a small saucepan over low heat. Cook, stirring constantly, until sugar has dissolved. Remove from heat and let stand 30 minutes. Process in blender until smooth. Taste and adjust seasonings.

Combine the beans, onions, and red hot chili pepper and stir in the dressing. Cover and allow to marinate for 1 hour. When well marinated, stir in ham and green peppers. Pour into a serving bowl and garnish with quartered hard-boiled eggs and chopped black olives, if desired.

Chilled Caribbean Shrimp Salad, on a bed of lettuce.

CHAPTER FOUR

MAIN COURSES

TRADITIONAL NEW ENGLAND SALMON WITH PEAS AND POTATOES ❦ PASTA WITH PEAS

FILLET OF BEEF WITH BLACK BEAN CHUTNEY ❦ TORTILLA AND BEAN TOWER

SOUTHWESTERN BEEF STEW ❦ MEXICAN HOT SUPPER ❦ CHILI AND ITS VARIATIONS

FEIJOADA ❦ BRUNSWICK STEW ❦ GRILLED RED SNAPPER WITH RED LENTIL SALSA

CHICK-PEA STEW ❦ SEARED SALMON WITH BLACK BEAN SCALLION SAUCE

GRILLED TUNA WITH PAPAYA VINIAGRETTE AND BLACK BEAN SALSA

WHITE BEAN GNOCCHI WITH PANCETTA AND CREAM ❦ CLAMS WITH BLACK BEAN SAUCE

MAMA'S PASTA ❦ BRAISED LAMB SHANKS WITH BEANS AND FENNEL ❦ BEANS ON TOAST

COUSCOUS ❦ BEAN RISOTTO WITH BAKED ITALIAN SAUSAGE ❦ SIMPLE CASSOULET

SHRIMP WITH ROSEMARIED BEANS AND TOMATOES ❦ LAMB TARTARE WITH HERBED WHITE BEANS

LENTIL CASSEROLE ❦ PICADILLO ❦ BLACK-EYED PEAS AND MEATBALLS

VEAL ROAST WITH FAVA BEANS ❦ BEAN LOAF WITH FRESH TOMATO SAUCES

TRADITIONAL NEW ENGLAND SALMON WITH PEAS AND POTATOES

SERVES 6 TO 8

1	*6-pound salmon, cleaned, head and tail removed*
1	*tablespoon fresh lemon juice*
10	*Romaine lettuce leaves*
3	*scallions, trimmed*
	James's Egg Sauce*
	Peas and Potatoes*
½	*cup chopped fresh parsley*

Preheat oven to 400°F.

Place salmon on a piece of heavy-duty aluminum foil large enough to enclose fish. Sprinkle with lemon juice and cover with lettuce leaves. Place scallions on top and enclose fish with foil, making sure that it is sealed. Place on a baking sheet in a preheated oven and bake for about 20 minutes or until salmon is just cooked. (Alternatively, you may grill salmon.) Remove from oven and let stand 5 minutes.

Carefully remove salmon from foil and place on a warm serving platter. Coat with James's Egg Sauce* and surround with Peas and Potatoes*. Sprinkle with parsley and serve immediately.

JAMES'S EGG SAUCE

MAKES 2 CUPS OF SAUCE

3	*tablespoons butter*
3	*tablespoons all-purpose flour*
	Salt to taste
	White pepper to taste
	Pinch ground nutmeg
1½	*cups warm heavy cream*
2	*hard-boiled eggs, chopped*

Heat butter in a heavy saucepan over medium heat. Blend in flour and seasonings. When well blended, whisk in warm cream and cook, stirring constantly, for 4 minutes or until thick. Remove from heat and stir in eggs. Keep warm until ready to serve.

PEAS AND POTATOES

SERVES 6

2 cups shelled fresh peas

¼ cup clarified butter

1 tablespoon chopped fresh mint

1 tablespoon chopped fresh dill

20 cooked small red potatoes

Salt to taste

Pepper to taste

Place peas in rapidly boiling salted water and cook for about 1 minute or until peas are just tender. Drain well.

Heat butter in heavy sauté pan over medium heat. Add chopped mint and dill and sauté for 2 minutes. Add potatoes and peas and continue to cook for about 3 minutes or until flavors are blended and vegetables are heated through. Taste and add additional salt and pepper if necessary.

PASTA WITH PEAS

SERVES 6

¼ pound prosciutto, finely julienned

2 cups shelled fresh peas or frozen petite peas

1½ pounds pasta of choice (cheese tortellini is particularly good)

2 cups heavy cream

¾ cup freshly grated Parmesan cheese

Salt to taste

White pepper to taste

Place prosciutto in a small sauté pan over medium heat and sauté, stirring frequently, for 5 minutes or until slightly crisp. Remove from pan and drain on a paper towel.

Place peas in rapidly boiling salted water and cook for about 1 minute or until just tender. Drain well. (Or if you are using frozen peas, defrost by placing them in a sieve under cold running water. When thawed, set aside to drain.)

Place pasta in a large pot of boiling salted water and cook according to directions for al dente. Drain well and return to pot.

While pasta is cooking, place cream in heavy saucepan over medium-high heat. When boiling, immediately reduce heat and simmer for about 5 minutes or until slightly thick. Pour warm cream over cooked pasta. Add prosciutto, peas, and Parmesan cheese. Return to low heat and cook for about 3 minutes or until sauce is thickened. Season with salt and white pepper and serve hot.

FILLET OF BEEF WITH BLACK BEAN CHUTNEY

SERVES 6 TO 8

1	fillet of beef, approximately 4 pounds, well trimmed and tied
2	tablespoons olive oil
	Salt to taste
	Pepper to taste
	Black Bean Chutney*

Preheat oven to 500°F.

Season fillet with olive oil and salt and pepper. Place baking sheet in preheated oven for 3 minutes or until very hot. When hot, place seasoned fillet on baking sheet. Lower heat to 450°F and roast for 12 minutes. Turn and roast other side for 12 minutes for rare meat. (Or roast to desired degree of doneness using a meat thermometer.)

Remove from oven and let stand for 10 minutes before slicing. Carve into ½-inch slices. Arrange down the center of a warm serving platter. Garnish with Black Bean Chutney* down each side of meat and serve immediately.

BLACK BEAN CHUTNEY

MAKES 8 CUPS OF CHUTNEY

5	cups chopped red onions
3	tablespoons minced garlic
1	jalapeño pepper, seeded and minced
½	cup fresh lemon juice
2	teaspoons whole cumin seeds
1	teaspoon whole mustard seeds
¼	cup light brown sugar
2	cups cooked, well-drained, dried black beans (see page 15)
1	cup diced jicama
¼	cup chopped fresh cilantro

Combine onions, garlic, jalapeño pepper, lemon juice, cumin and mustard seeds, and brown sugar in a heavy saucepan over medium heat. Bring to a boil, stirring frequently. Boil for 5 minutes, stirring continuously. Remove from heat and stir in black beans, jicama, and cilantro. Set aside and let marinate for at least 1 hour before using.

Any leftover chutney may be stored, covered and refrigerated, for up to 2 weeks.

Hearty Fillet of Beef with Black Bean Chutney.

TORTILLA AND BEAN TOWER
SERVES 6 TO 8

2 cups dried pinto or other red beans

2 tablespoons canola oil

1 cup chopped onions

2 tablespoons minced garlic

2 cups drained and chopped canned plum tomatoes

1 cup tomato paste

1 tablespoon chopped fresh epazote

1 tablespoon minced fresh parsley

1 teaspoon chopped fresh mint

2 tablespoons chili powder

1 teaspoon ground cumin

1½ cups cooked hominy

1 cup pitted black olives, chopped

 Salt to taste

 Pepper to taste

 Tabasco to taste

 Approximately 16 corn tortillas

3 cups grated Monterey Jack cheese

1 cup grated jalapeño jack cheese

1½ cups chopped seedless tomatoes

2 cups shredded iceberg lettuce

1½ cups chopped avocado

1 cup chopped pickled green chili peppers

Soak, rinse, and cook beans (see page 15). When beans are just tender, remove from heat and set aside.

Preheat oven to 375°F.

Generously line a 4-quart casserole with double-thickness, heavy-duty aluminum foil, leaving at least a 2-inch edge by which you can lift the finished bean tower out of the casserole. Generously oil foil and set aside.

Heat oil in a deep saucepan over medium-high heat. When hot, add onions and garlic and sauté for 4 minutes or until soft. Stir in tomatoes, tomato paste, herbs, and spices and continue cooking for about 15 minutes or until tomato sauce begins to thicken. Add beans, hominy, and olives and continue cooking for 15 minutes. Remove from heat. Stir in salt, pepper, and Tabasco.

Line the prepared casserole with corn tortillas to cover bottom and sides. Using a slotted spoon, cover bottom with a 1-inch layer of beans. Then cover with a layer of Monterey Jack cheese and a layer of tortillas. Continue making layers until casserole is filled up to about three-quarters of an inch from the top, ending with beans.

Place in preheated oven and bake for 30 minutes or until bubbling. Remove from oven and cover top with jalapeño jack cheese and chopped fried tortillas. (To do this, heat 2 tablespoons of fat over medium-high heat. Fry each tortilla for one minute per side until crisp. Drain on a paper towel and chop.) Return to oven for 5 minutes or until cheese has melted. Remove from oven and let stand in a warm spot for 30 minutes.

Lift the tortilla tower out of the casserole by holding onto the foil. Invert onto a warm serving platter and gently peel away the foil. Surround tower with tomatoes, lettuce, avocado, and pickled chili peppers. Serve immediately.

SOUTHWESTERN BEEF STEW

SERVES 6 TO 8

3   *pounds lean stewing beef, cut into 1½ inch cubes*

1   *cup all-purpose flour*

    Salt to taste

    Pepper to taste

3   *tablespoons vegetable oil*

2   *cups diced onions*

4   *cloves garlic, peeled and chopped*

½   *cup diced green bell peppers*

½   *teaspoon minced fresh oregano*

½   *teaspoon minced fresh mint*

1   *tablespoon ground cumin*

1   *tablespoon chili powder*

    Cayenne to taste

1   *cup chopped canned green chili peppers, well drained*

1   *jalapeño pepper, seeded and chopped*

2   *cups chopped canned Italian plum tomatoes with juice*

1   *bottle dark beer*

2   *cups cooked, drained, dried black or pinto beans (see page 15)*

2   *cups cooked corn kernels*

1½   *cups grated Monterey Jack cheese*

Preheat oven to 375°F.

Dredge beef in flour and salt and pepper. Set aside.

Heat 2 tablespoons oil in Dutch oven over medium-high heat. When hot, brown the meat in batches, turning to sear all sides. Remove browned beef to a paper towel to drain. When all beef has been browned, add remaining oil to pan. Stir in onions, garlic, and bell peppers and sauté, stirring frequently, for about 5 minutes or until onions are just soft. Return meat to pan. Stir in herbs, spices, green chili and jalapeño peppers, tomatoes, and beer. Cook for 10 minutes, stirring frequently. Cover and bake in preheated oven for 1½ hours until meat is very tender. Remove from oven and stir in beans and corn. Return to oven uncovered for 15 minutes. Serve hot in large soup bowls sprinkled with Monterey Jack cheese.

© Steven Mark Needham/Envision

MEXICAN HOT SUPPER
SERVES 6

3   *cups cooked, drained, dried pinto or other red beans (see page 15)*

4   *cups cooked rice (brown or white)*

1   *cup sour cream*

¼   *cup diced red bell peppers*

¼   *cup diced green bell peppers*

¼   *cup diced pickled jalapeño peppers*

1   *tablespoon chili powder*

1   *teaspoon ground cumin*

¼   *teaspoon ground oregano*

1   *teaspoon chopped fresh mint*

    Tabasco to taste

    Salt to taste

    Pepper to taste

3   *large eggs*

2   *cups milk*

1   *cup drained, sliced, canned green chili peppers*

1½   *cup grated Monterey Jack or jalapeño cheese*

¾   *cup grated sharp cheddar cheese*

Preheat oven to 350°F.

Generously grease a 3-quart casserole and set aside.

Combine beans, rice, sour cream, bell peppers, pickled jalapeño peppers, chili powder, cumin, oregano, mint, Tabasco, and salt and pepper.

Beat eggs and milk together and set aside.

Place one-third of the bean mixture in the bottom of the prepared casserole. Sprinkle with half of the sliced green chili peppers and then cover with a layer of Monterey Jack or jalapeño cheese. Pour 1 cup of the egg and milk mixture over the top. Repeat with another layer of beans, chili peppers, cheese, and 1 cup of the egg and milk mixture and then with a final layer of beans. Pour remaining egg and milk mixture on top and allow to soak in.

Place in the preheated oven and bake for about 35 minutes or until bubbly. Five minutes before the casserole is ready, sprinkle cheddar cheese on top and bake for the remaining time. Serve hot.

CHILI AND ITS VARIATIONS
SERVES 6 TO 8

1   *pound dried pinto, pink, or red kidney beans*

2   *dried red hot chili peppers*

2   *tablespoons peanut oil or other vegetable oil*

2   *cups chopped onions*

1   *tablespoon minced garlic*

2   *green bell peppers, seeded and chopped*

1   *jalapeño pepper, seeded and minced (or to taste)*

2   *tablespoons masa harina*

¼   *cup fine chili powder*

1   *tablespoon ground cumin (or more to taste)*

1   *tablespoon cocoa powder*

¼   *teaspoon ground cinnamon*

½   *teaspoon ground turmeric*

½   *teaspoon ground oregano (or to taste)*

4   *cups canned tomatoes with juice*

1   *cup tomato sauce*

     Tabasco to taste

     Salt to taste

     Pepper to taste

Soak, rinse, and cook beans (see page 15).

Soak dried red hot chili peppers in hot water to cover for 15 minutes. When soft, remove from water and chop. Set aside.

Heat oil in heavy sauté pan over medium-high heat. When hot, add onions. Lower heat to medium-low and sauté onions for 5 minutes. Add garlic and sauté for an additional 2 minutes. Add bell, jalapeño, and dried chili peppers. Continue to sauté for 4 more minutes. Stir in masa harina, chili powder, cumin, cocoa, cinnamon, turmeric, and oregano. When well blended, stir in about 1 cup of liquid from the beans and continue stirring to remove any bits from the pan. Scrape contents of sauté pan into beans. Add tomatoes, tomato sauce, Tabasco, and salt and pepper.

Place over medium-high heat and bring to a boil. When boiling, lower heat and simmer for about 30 minutes or until flavors are well blended. Serve hot.

Variations:

1. For chili con carne: After onions and garlic are sautéed, add 2 pounds of coarsely ground beef, veal, or turkey or 2 pounds very lean beef, pork, or venison stew meat cut into 1-inch cubes, or 2 pounds game or other rich sausage links. Sauté for 10 minutes or until meat begins to brown. Continue with master recipe.

2. For vegetarian chili: When adding tomatoes, add 6 cups chopped mixed fresh vegetables such as carrots, red bell peppers, celery, squash, hominy, and if desired, ½ pound tofu cut into ½-inch cubes.

3. All chili variations may be garnished with one or a combination of the following: crisp tortilla chips, sour cream, grated cheese, chopped cilantro, chopped onions, shredded lettuce, lime slices, and pickled hot peppers.

FEIJOADA
SERVES 8 TO 10

2 cups dried black beans

4 cups chicken or beef stock

1 3-pound smoked beef tongue, skinned and well trimmed

2 pounds chorizo (or kielbasa)

2 pounds beef brisket, trimmed of fat

2 pig's feet, cleaned and halved

1 pound salt pork, diced

2 tablespoons bacon fat or vegetable oil

2 cups chopped onions

2 tablespoons minced garlic

2 jalapeño peppers, seeded and minced (or to taste)

4 cups chopped canned Italian plum tomatoes with juice

   Peel of 1 large orange

2 bay leaves

   Salt to taste

   Pepper to taste

10 cups warm, cooked white rice

4 seedless oranges, peeled and sliced

   Spicy Lime Sauce*

Soak beans (see page 15).

Bring 8 cups water and stock to boil in a stockpot. When boiling, add beans, beef tongue, chorizo, brisket, pig's feet, and salt pork. Bring to a boil, then lower heat to a simmer and cook for 45 minutes.

Heat bacon fat or oil in a heavy sauté pan over high heat. Add onions, garlic, and jalapeño pepper. Sauté 5 minutes. Add tomatoes, orange peel, bay leaves, salt, and pepper. Lower heat, simmer for 20 minutes.

When beans have cooked for 45 minutes, remove about 2 cups with some broth. Mash them and stir them into the tomatoes. When well combined, add the tomato mixture to the stockpot. Cook for another hour or until meats are very well done. If the beans get too thick, add more stock as they should remain fairly soupy. Remove the bay leaves and orange peel.

Remove meats and slice into bite-size pieces. Place on a serving platter around a mound of white rice. Pour beans into a large bowl. Serve immediately with sliced oranges and Spicy Lime Sauce*.

SPICY LIME SAUCE
MAKES APPROXIMATELY 3 CUPS OF SAUCE

1½ pounds fresh plum tomatoes, peeled, cored, and seeded

1 jalapeño pepper (or to taste)

1 cup chopped red onions

1 tablespoon chopped garlic

2 teaspoons chopped fresh cilantro

½ cup fresh lime juice

¼ cup fresh orange juice

½ cup olive oil

Combine all ingredients in a food processor fitted with the metal blade, using quick on-and-off turns. Set aside to marinate for at least 1 hour before using. The unused sauce can be stored, covered, in the refrigerator, for up to one week.

BRUNSWICK STEW

SERVES 6

1   cup all-purpose flour

1   teaspoon paprika

   Salt to taste

   Pepper to taste

5   pounds stewing chicken: breast, legs, and thighs

½   cup clarified butter or vegetable oil

1   cup diced onions

½   cup diced green bell peppers

2   tablespoons minced fresh parsley

1   teaspoon minced fresh thyme

1   teaspoon minced fresh sage

1   teaspoon minced fresh dill

2   cups well-drained canned Italian plum tomatoes

2   cups chicken stock

2   cups water

2   cups fresh lima beans (thawed frozen may be substituted)

2   cups fresh yellow corn kernels (thawed frozen may be substituted)

2   cups diced Idaho potatoes, skin on (optional)

Combine flour, paprika, salt, and pepper. Dredge chicken pieces in seasoned flour.

Heat butter or oil in Dutch oven over medium heat. When hot, brown chicken pieces in batches, turning to brown all sides. Drain browned chicken pieces on a paper towel and set aside.

When all chicken has browned, pour off all but 2 tablespoons fat. Stir in onions, bell pepper, parsley, thyme, sage, and dill. Sauté, stirring frequently, for about 5 minutes or until vegetables are quite soft. Return chicken to the Dutch oven. Add tomatoes, chicken stock, and water. Cover, raise heat, and bring to a boil. When boiling, lower heat and simmer for 30 minutes or until chicken is just cooked. Add additional chicken stock if necessary. Add lima beans, corn, and potato, if desired. Taste and adjust seasoning. Cover and raise heat to bring again to a boil.

When boiling, lower heat to a simmer and cook for an additional 20 minutes or until vegetables are cooked and flavors are well combined. Serve hot.

Variation:

Add 2 cups okra when you add the corn and lima beans.

GRILLED RED SNAPPER WITH RED LENTIL SALSA

SERVES 6

2	*cups cooked, drained, red lentils (see page 15)*
¾	*cup finely diced green bell peppers*
½	*cup finely diced yellow bell peppers*
½	*cup finely diced skinless, seedless, yellow tomatoes*
¼	*cup finely diced shallots*
¾	*cup minced fresh cilantro*
½	*teaspoon curry powder*
½	*teaspoon ground cumin*
	Salt to taste
	Pepper to taste
2	*tablespoons sherry wine vinegar*
¼	*cup olive oil*
6	*8-ounce skinless red snapper fillets, well trimmed of fat*
6	*generous lime wedges*

Combine lentils, bell peppers, tomatoes, shallots, ¼ cup cilantro, spices, vinegar, and 2 tablespoons oil. Stir to combine and set aside at room temperature to marinate for 1 hour.

Rub remaining olive oil on red snapper fillets and season with salt and pepper, if desired.

Prepare grill. (Or place fish on a baking sheet covered with oil, foil, or parchment paper. Place in a 450°F oven for about 8 minutes or until fish is just done.)

When grill is hot, place fish on grill for about 4 minutes per side or until done to desired degree.

Place a generous scoop of salsa on warm serving plates and place a grilled fillet in the center. Sprinkle with remaining cilantro and garnish with a lime wedge. Serve immediately.

Grilled Red Snapper with Red Lentil Salsa, trimmed with parsley and limes.

CHICK-PEA STEW
SERVES 6

2	tablespoons olive oil
2	cups diced onions
2	tablespoons minced garlic
3	cups sliced wild mushrooms
1½	cups diced carrots
1	cinnamon stick broken into pieces
4	cloves
1	teaspoon white peppercorns
½	teaspoon allspice berries (whole allspice)
2	cups canned plum tomatoes, well drained
	Salt to taste
	Pepper to taste
4	cups cooked, well-drained, dried chick-peas (see page 15)
½	cup pitted Greek olives, drained
1	teaspoon minced fresh thyme
½	cup minced fresh parsley
1	tablespoon fresh lemon juice

Heat oil in large, heavy saucepan over medium-high heat. When hot, add onions and garlic. Lower heat and sauté for 4 minutes or until vegetables are just soft. Stir in mushrooms and carrots and sauté for 5 minutes.

Tie cinnamon stick, cloves, peppercorns, and allspice berries in a small cheesecloth bag. Add to vegetables with the tomatoes and salt and pepper. Bring to a simmer and cook for 15 minutes or until vegetables are just soft. Stir in chick-peas, olives, thyme, and ¼ cup parsley and cook for an additional 15 minutes. Stir in lemon juice and remaining parsley. Remove cheesecloth. Serve hot with brown rice, if desired.

SEARED SALMON WITH BLACK BEAN SCALLION SAUCE
SERVES 6

6	7-ounce salmon fillets, trimmed of any skin
	Salt to taste
	White pepper to taste
2	tablespoons safflower oil
	Black Bean Scallion Sauce*
6	Scallion Brushes*
2	tablespoons chopped chives

Season salmon with salt and white pepper. Heat oil in heavy sauté pan over medium heat. When hot, add fish and cook for about 4 minutes or until fish is almost cooked through. Turn and cook for 2 minutes. (You may also grill the fillet.)

Place some Black Bean Scallion Sauce* on one side of a serving plate. Lay a Scallion Brush* at the top. Place salmon fillet so top edge covers center of Scallion Brush. Sprinkle with chives and serve immediately.

BLACK BEAN SCALLION SAUCE

MAKES APPROXIMATELY 4¼ CUPS OF SAUCE

1	*tablespoon safflower oil*
¼	*cup minced scallions, white part only*
1	*tablespoon minced shallots*
2	*teaspoons minced fresh ginger*
1	*teaspoon minced garlic*
2	*cups cooked dried black beans (see page 15)*
2	*cups fresh chicken stock*
¼	*cup fresh orange juice*
1	*tablespoon fresh lime juice*
	Dash ground cinnamon
	Salt to taste
	Pepper to taste

Heat oil in medium saucepan over medium-high heat. When hot, add scallions, shallots, ginger, and garlic. Lower heat and cook for about 3 minutes or until vegetables are soft. Add remaining ingredients and raise heat to medium. Cook, stirring frequently, for about 15 minutes or until reduced by one-half.

When reduced, remove from heat and pour into a food processor fitted with the metal blade. Puree until smooth. Taste and adjust seasoning, if necessary.

SCALLION BRUSHES

6	*firm scallions of the same size*
	Cold water
6	*ice cubes*

Trim both ends from scallions to make six uniform pieces, 4½ inches long. Lay each piece out on a cutting board and make even crosscuts 1 inch deep on each end so that each end has numerous shards. When all six scallions have been cut, cover with cold water and ice and let sit for at least 10 minutes or until the ends open up to form brushes. Drain well and dry.

GRILLED TUNA WITH PAPAYA VINAIGRETTE AND BLACK BEAN SALSA
SERVES 6

6   7-ounce tuna steaks, well trimmed

2   tablespoons extra virgin olive oil

1   tablespoon fresh lime juice

   Salt to taste

   Pepper to taste

   Papaya Vinaigrette*

   Black Bean Salsa*

Prepare grill or preheat broiler.

Combine olive oil and lime juice and generously brush onto each tuna steak. Season with salt and pepper. Place on hot grill and grill each side for about 3 minutes or until just cooked.

Place a pool of Papaya Vinaigrette* on warm dinner plates. Lay a tuna steak on top. Drizzle on the remaining vinaigrette and garnish with Black Bean Salsa*.

PAPAYA VINAIGRETTE
MAKES 1½ CUPS

1   very ripe papaya, peeled and seeded

1   tablespoon fresh lime juice

1   shallot, peeled and minced

1   teaspoon minced fresh mint

¼   cup fresh orange juice

½   cup dry white wine

½   cup peanut oil

   Salt to taste

   White pepper to taste

Puree papaya and lime juice in a food processor fitted with the metal blade.

Combine shallot, mint, orange juice, and white wine in a small saucepan over medium heat. Bring to a boil. Boil for about 5 minutes or until liquid has reduced by half.

Pour papaya puree in food processor bowl and process until well blended. Pour into a small mixing bowl and whisk in peanut oil. Season with salt and pepper. Cover and set aside until ready to use.

BLACK BEAN SALSA
MAKES 4 CUPS OF SALSA

2   *cups cooked and drained dried black beans (see page 15)*

½   *cup minced fresh tomatillos*

½   *cup diced red onions*

¼   *cup diced yellow bell peppers*

¼   *cup diced green bell peppers*

¼   *cup diced red bell peppers*

1   *jalapeño pepper, seeded and minced*

2   *shallots, peeled and minced*

1   *clove garlic, peeled and minced*

1   *tablespoon white wine vinegar*

2   *teaspoons fresh lime juice*

Salt to taste

Pepper to taste

Combine all ingredients. Cover and refrigerate for at least 1 hour before using. Taste and adjust seasonings before use.

WHITE BEAN GNOCCHI WITH PANCETTA AND CREAM
SERVES 6

1   *pound pancetta, diced*

3   *cups cooked, mashed, dried white beans (see page 15)*

1   *egg*

Approximately 1 cup all-purpose flour

¼   *teaspoon salt (or to taste)*

1   *cup grated Parmesan cheese*

1½   *cups warm heavy cream*

Place pancetta in a heavy sauté pan over medium heat. Cook, stirring frequently, for about 10 minutes or until quite crisp. Drain on a paper towel and set aside.

Place the beans in a heavy saucepan over high heat. Quickly move the beans around the pan for about 2 minutes or until beans begin to dry. Do not allow them to brown. Remove from heat and cool.

Combine cooled beans with egg, approximately ¾ cup flour, and salt to make a light dough. Sprinkle some of the flour on a clean, cool work surface. Roll a handful of dough out on the floured surface to make a long, finger-size roll. Cut into 1-inch pieces. Continue with remaining dough to make more pieces.

Place gnocchi, a few at a time, in rapidly boiling salted water. Cook for about 3 minutes or until gnocchis rise to the surface. Remove with a slotted spoon and keep warm.

When all gnocchi are cooked, toss with pancetta, Parmesan cheese, and warm cream. Serve hot with additional cheese, if desired.

CLAMS WITH BLACK BEAN SAUCE

SERVES 6

Approximately 4 pounds coarse salt

36   *large freshly shucked clams on the half shell*

2   *tablespoons fermented black beans (Available at Asian markets, gourmet shops, and some supermarkets.)*

3   *cloves garlic, peeled and minced*

⅓   *cup chopped scallions*

1   *teaspoon minced fresh ginger*

1   *tablespoon minced red hot chili peppers (or to taste)*

1   *teaspoon orange zest*

½   *cup Shao Hsing wine (available at Asian markets and gourmet shops) or dry sherry*

½   *cup chicken stock*

3   *tablespoons fresh orange juice*

2   *teaspoons sugar*

3   *tablespoons vegetable oil*

2   *teaspoons sesame oil*

4   *cups cooked white rice (optional), or*

4   *cups cooked pasta (optional)*

Preheat oven to 500°F.

Place a ½-inch layer of coarse salt on a baking sheet with sides. Set clams into the salt.

Chop the black beans and combine with remaining ingredients. Place in a medium-sized saucepan over medium heat and cook for 5 minutes. Remove from heat and spoon bean sauce over each clam. Seal pan with aluminum foil. Bake for 5 minutes or until clams just begin to curl. Serve with white rice or pasta.

MAMA'S PASTA

SERVES 6

1   *pound sweet Italian sausage*

1   *pound hot Italian sausage*

1   *cup chopped onions*

1   *tablespoon minced garlic*

¼   *cup minced fresh Italian parsley*

¾   *cup dry white wine*

5   *cups canned Italian plum tomatoes with juice*

Salt to taste

Pepper to taste

1   *package rigatoni, bow ties, penne, rotelle, or spaghetti*

2   *cups cooked, drained, fresh cannellini, Great Northern, or fava beans (see page 15)*

1½   *cups chopped bitter greens (such as arugula or chicory)*

1   *cup freshly grated Parmesan cheese*

Crumble sausages into heavy sauté pan over medium heat. Stir in onions, garlic, and parsley and sauté, stirring frequently, for about 15 minutes or until sausage is cooked. Add white wine and tomatoes and cook for about 30 minutes or until sauce is well flavored. Add salt and pepper.

Cook pasta in rapidly boiling water according to package directions for al dente. When done, drain well. Return to pot and stir in sausage mixture, beans, and bitter greens. Return to heat to warm through. Serve with grated Parmesan cheese.

Mama's Pasta, home cooking at its best!

BRAISED LAMB SHANKS WITH BEANS AND FENNEL
SERVES 6

1   pound cranberry, Jacob's cattle, tongues of fire, or other mottled dried beans

1   cup all-purpose flour

    Salt to taste

    Pepper to taste

1   teaspoon paprika

8   lamb shanks, split

3   tablespoons olive oil

2   cups sliced leeks, white part only

1   cup chopped celery

1   cup chopped carrots

½   cup chopped parsnips

1½   cups dark beer

1½   cups vegetable, beef, or chicken stock, or a combination of the three

2   tablespoons tomato paste

1   teaspoon minced fresh thyme

1   teaspoon minced fresh marjoram

½   teaspoon minced fresh sage

2   tablespoons minced fresh Italian parsley

1   tablespoon lemon juice

    Braised Fennel*

Soak, rinse, and cook beans (see page 15). When tender, remove from heat and set aside.

Season flour with salt, pepper, and paprika. Toss lamb shanks in seasoned flour to coat well. Heat 2 tablespoons oil in heavy Dutch oven with lid over medium-high heat. When hot, add floured lamb shanks and cook, turning frequently, for about 7 minutes or until all sides are browned. Remove shanks from heat and drain excess grease onto a paper towel. Transfer shanks to a platter and set aside.

Carefully wipe grease from Dutch oven. Return to heat and add remaining oil. When hot, add leeks, celery, carrots, and parsnips. Sauté for 5 minutes or until vegetables begin to brown. Stir in beer, stock, tomato paste, and herbs. Raise heat and bring to a boil. When boiling, lower heat to a simmer and cook for 10 minutes. Then add lamb and its accumulated juices. Again raise heat and bring to a boil. When boiling, lower heat to a simmer, cover, and simmer for about 1 hour. Remove cover and cook for another 30 minutes or until gravy has begun to thicken.

Preheat oven to 350°F.

Mash 2 cups cooked beans and stir into lamb shanks along with lemon juice. Taste and adjust seasoning. Cover top of lamb shanks with remaining beans. Nestle Braised Fennel* around the edges. Place in preheated oven and bake for 20 minutes. Remove from heat and serve immediately.

BRAISED FENNEL

4   *hearts of fennel, quartered*

2   *tablespoons extra virgin olive oil*

      Juice and zest of 1 lemon

¼   *cup white wine*

¼   *cup chicken broth*

Preheat oven to 350°F.

Combine fennel with olive oil and lemon juice and zest. Bring wine and broth to a boil in a heavy skillet over high heat. When boiling, add fennel and stir to coat.

Place in preheated oven and bake for about 25 minutes or until fennel is very tender and nicely browned. Serve warm.

BEANS ON TOAST

SERVES 6

12   *slices very lean bacon*

6   *slices whole-grain bread, lightly toasted*

3   *tablespoons honey mustard or another mustard of your choice (or to taste)*

4   *cups warm Boston Baked Beans**

1   *cup grated cheddar cheese or cheese of your choice*

Preheat broiler.

Place bacon slices in frying pan over medium heat. When bacon begins to sizzle, lower heat and continue to cook for approximately 4 minutes or until bacon is cooked but not yet crisp. Remove from heat and drain bacon on a paper towel.

Generously coat toasted bread with mustard. Mound warm baked beans on toast and sprinkle with grated cheese. Crisscross bacon strips over each piece of bread.

Place in preheated broiler and cook for approximately 3 minutes or until cheese has melted and bacon has crisped.

Remove from heat and serve immediately with coleslaw if desired.

COUSCOUS
SERVES 6

1½	cups couscous
3	cups boiling water
	Salt to taste
3	tablespoons olive oil
1	teaspoon ground cinnamon
2	cups carrot chunks
2	cups squash chunks
1	cup parsnip chunks
1	cup cauliflower florets
1	cup potato chunks
1	cup onion chunks
2	cups cooked, drained, chick-peas
	Tomato Sauce*
	Harissa*

Line the top half of a large vegetable steamer with cheesecloth. Set aside.

Combine couscous, boiling water, and salt in a heatproof bowl. Allow to soak 15 minutes. Pour off any remaining water and rub grains with your fingers to eliminate lumps. Stir in olive oil and cinnamon. Place couscous in prepared vegetable steamer over boiling water. Arrange vegetables and beans over couscous. Cover and steam for 30 minutes or until vegetables are done and couscous is tender.

Transfer to a hot serving platter and cover with Tomato Sauce*. Serve Harissa* on the side.

Exotic Couscous served with Harissa.

TOMATO SAUCE
MAKES 4 CUPS OF SAUCE

4	cups skinless, seedless, diced ripe tomatoes
1	jalapeño pepper, seeded and minced
	Salt to taste
1	tablespoon sugar or maple syrup

Place all ingredients in a heavy saucepan over medium heat and simmer for about 15 minutes or until tomatoes are very soft. Serve warm.

HARISSA

6	dried red hot chili peppers, stemmed
6	serrano chili peppers, stemmed
4	cloves garlic
2	scallions, trimmed and chopped
½	teaspoon ground cumin
½	teaspoon caraway seed
½	teaspoon ground coriander
⅓	cup olive oil

Soak red peppers and serrano peppers in boiling water to cover for 1 hour or until quite soft. When soft, drain. Place in a food processor with remaining ingredients. Process until well combined, but do not puree. Cover and refrigerate until ready to use.

For a less fiery sauce, seed and devein the chilies before use. When doing so, wear rubber gloves and avoid contact with eyes, as chili peppers can burn.

BEAN RISOTTO
WITH BAKED ITALIAN SAUSAGE
SERVES 6

1	*pound dried beans (any type except black beans may be used)*
5	*cups chicken stock*
½	*cup chopped onions*
½	*cup grated carrots*
¼	*pound chopped raw bacon*
2	*cups drained and chopped canned Italian plum tomatoes*
12	*Italian sausages, hot or sweet or a combination of the two*
1	*cup sun-dried tomatoes packed in oil*
1	*cup sliced red onions*
1	*cup sliced green bell peppers*
2	*tablespoons olive oil*
½	*teaspoon minced fresh rosemary*
½	*teaspoon minced fresh sage*
½	*teaspoon minced fresh thyme*
1½	*cups Arborio rice*
¼	*cup dry white wine*
½	*cup grated Parmesan cheese*

Soak beans (see page 15). Place in large saucepan with 4 cups chicken stock, onions, carrots, and bacon. Bring to a boil and cook for about 1 hour until beans are tender. Add tomatoes and remaining stock. Bring to a boil. Remove from heat and set aside.

Preheat oven to 400°F.

Place sausage on baking tray with sun-dried tomatoes, red onions, and bell peppers. Place in preheated oven and bake for 30 minutes or until sausages are browned and fully cooked. Set aside and keep warm.

Heat olive oil and herbs in heavy saucepan over medium heat. Add rice and stir for about 2 minutes or until rice is glistening. Add white wine and cook, stirring constantly, until wine is absorbed. Pour in ½ cup bean liquid and cook, stirring frequently, until liquid is absorbed. Continue adding ½ cup bean liquid at a time and stir until risotto is creamy and tender. Stir in 1 cup drained beans and Parmesan cheese.

Place risotto in the center of a large, warm serving platter. Scoop beans from cooking liquid with a slotted spoon and place around risotto. Place sausages on beans and serve immediately.

BEAN LOAF WITH FRESH TOMATO SAUCE

SERVES 6

1   *pound dried beans of choice*

1   *cup chopped carrots*

½   *cup chopped onions*

½   *cup chopped celery*

3   *large eggs*

2   *tablespoons milk*

1½   *cups fresh bread crumbs or cooked brown rice*

2   *tablespoons melted butter*

1   *tablespoon fresh lemon juice*

     Tabasco to taste

     Salt to taste

     Pepper to taste

     *Fresh Tomato Sauce**

Soak, rinse, and cook beans as directed (see page 15). When cooked, drain beans, reserving the liquid.

Preheat oven to 350°F.

Grease a 3-quart loaf pan or terrine and set aside.

Finely chop carrots, onions, and celery in a food processor fitted with the metal blade. Add beans and process until smooth. Scrape from processor bowl into a mixing bowl. Stir in eggs, milk, bread crumbs or rice, butter, lemon juice, and seasonings. Mixture should be fairly stiff. If not, add additional bread crumbs or rice.

Pour into prepared pan. Place in preheated oven and bake for about 1 hour or until top is brown and edges have begun to pull away from pan. If the top browns too quickly, cover with aluminum foil. Remove from oven and let stand for 15 minutes.

Invert and tap from pan and cut into ½-inch slices. Place on a warm serving platter and cover with Fresh Tomato Sauce*, passing additonal sauce on the side. This may be served either hot or cold.

FRESH TOMATO SAUCE

MAKES 3 CUPS OF SAUCE

2   *tablespoons olive oil*

¼   *cup minced shallots*

3   *cups chopped, peeled, cored, and seeded very ripe tomatoes*

1   *teaspoon sugar*

     Salt to taste

     Pepper to taste

Heat olive oil in heavy sauté pan over medium heat. When hot, add shallots and sauté for 3 minutes or until just soft. Add tomatoes, sugar, and salt and pepper and simmer for 30 minutes or until slightly thick. Serve hot or cold.

CHAPTER FIVE

ACCOMPANIMENTS

RISI E BICI ❦ GREEN BEANS IN WALNUT BUTTER

GINGERED CHICK-PEAS ❦ SUMMER BEANS ❦ SUCCOTASH

CREAMED BEANS ❦ SESAME SNOW PEAS ❦ BEANS AGRO DOLCE

MINTED PEAS ❦ BEANS 'N GREENS ❦ BULGUR AND PEA PILAF

BOSTON BAKED BEANS ❦ GARLIC AND WHITE BEAN PUREE

FLORENTINE BEANS ❦ SOUR CREAM-BAKED LIMA BEANS

CUBAN BLACK BEANS (MOORS AND CHRISTIANS)

CREAMED NEW POTATOES AND PEAS ❦ DAL PANCAKES ❦ HOPPIN' JOHN

JALAPEÑO BEANS ❦ RED BEANS AND RICE ❦ REFRIED BEANS

RISI E BICI
SERVES 6

¼   teaspoon saffron threads

Approximately 4 cups very hot chicken stock

3   tablespoons unsalted butter

¼   cup chopped fresh fennel

¼   cup chopped onion

1   cup Arborio rice

½   cup dry white wine

2   cups shelled fresh peas (or 2 cups thawed frozen petite peas)

1   tablespoon extra virgin olive oil

1   cup grated Parmesan cheese

Freshly grated black pepper to taste

Place saffron in chicken broth and allow to steep while keeping broth warm.

Melt butter in a heavy saucepan over medium heat. When melted, stir in fennel and onion. Sauté for 3 minutes or until vegetables begin to soften. Add rice and cook, stirring frequently, for about 3 minutes or until rice is shiny and has begun to absorb the butter. Lower heat and pour in wine. Cook, stirring constantly, for about 4 minutes or until wine is absorbed. Pour in hot stock, about ¼ cup at a time, and continue to cook, stirring constantly, as each ¼ cup is absorbed and rice is creamy. Rice should remain chewy.

Stir in peas and olive oil and cook for an additional 3 minutes. Remove from heat and stir in ½ cup Parmesan cheese. Cover and let stand 5 minutes. Serve with remaining Parmesan cheese and freshly grated black pepper, if desired.

This recipe does not call for salt since chicken stock and Parmesan cheese generally add enough flavor. However, you may wish to taste before serving.

GREEN BEANS IN WALNUT BUTTER
SERVES 6

1½   pounds fresh green beans, trimmed

1   tablespoon clarified butter

1   teaspoon walnut oil

¼   cup chopped walnuts (black walnuts may be used)

1   tablespoon minced fresh basil

Salt to taste

Pepper to taste

Cook beans in rapidly boiling salted water for 3 minutes or until bright green and still crisp. Immediately shock under cold running water. When chilled, drain and pat dry.

Combine butter, walnut oil, and walnuts in a medium sauté pan over medium heat. Sauté for about 4 minutes or until walnuts are golden. Add basil and beans and toss to coat and heat through. Add salt and pepper and serve immediately.

Elegant Green Beans in Walnut Butter, dressed with fresh basil.

GINGERED CHICK-PEAS
SERVES 6

1   pound dried chick-peas

¼   cup peanut oil

2   cups chopped onions

1   cup peeled, cored, seeded, and chopped very ripe
     tomatoes

1   tablespoon grated fresh ginger

1   tablespoon minced garlic

1   chopped jalapeño pepper

1   tablespoon minced fresh basil

1   tablespoon minced fresh cilantro

1   tablespoon ground cumin

1   tablespoon garam masala (Available from Asian
     markets, specialty stores, and some supermarkets.)

1   teaspoon ground coriander

½   teaspoon cayenne (or to taste)

¼   cup fresh orange juice

2   tablespoons fresh lemon juice

     Grated zest of one orange

Soak, rinse, and cook chick-peas (see page 15). When cooked, drain and reserve liquid.

Heat oil in heavy saucepan over medium heat. When hot, add onion. Lower heat and sauté for about 10 minutes or until onions are beginning to get quite brown. Add tomatoes, ginger, garlic, jalapeño pepper, herbs, spices, orange juice, lemon juice, and orange zest. Continue to cook, stirring frequently, for about 15 minutes or until flavors are well blended.

Stir in chick-peas and continue to cook for another 15 minutes, adding bean cooking liquid as necessary. When beans are heated through, remove from heat and serve hot, or allow to cool to room temperature, then serve.

SUMMER BEANS
SERVES 6

¾   pound fresh green beans

¾   pound fresh yellow wax beans

     Salt to taste

1   tablespoon olive oil

¼   cup grated Parmesan cheese

1   tablespoon fresh minced parsley

     Fresh cracked pepper to taste

Wash and stem beans. Place in a medium-sized saucepan. Cover with water and add salt. Bring to a boil over high heat. Lower heat and cook for about 3 minutes or until beans are tender but still crisp. Drain and quickly pat dry.

Place in a serving bowl and add remaining ingredients. Stir to coat and serve immediately.

SUCCOTASH

SERVES 6

2   *cups fresh lima beans*

2   *tablespoons unsalted butter*

2   *cups cooked fresh corn kernels*

1   *cup peeled, cored, seeded, and diced tomatoes*

    Salt to taste

    Pepper to taste

Cook lima beans in rapidly boiling salted water for 5 minutes or until tender. Drain well.

Melt butter in heavy sauté pan over medium-low heat. Add beans, corn, and tomatoes. Cook, stirring frequently, for about 5 minutes or until flavors are combined. Add salt and pepper and serve hot.

Variations:

1. Use any variety of bean, cooked, dried, or fresh, combined with corn to make succotash.

2. Add ½ cup diced onions, ½ cup diced bell peppers, and ¼ cup cream in place of tomatoes, if desired, or in combination with tomatoes.

CREAMED BEANS

SERVES 6

1   *tablespoon butter*

1   *tablespoon all-purpose flour*

¾   *cup hot chicken stock*

¾   *cup heavy cream*

½   *teaspoon grated orange zest*

1   *teaspoon minced fresh basil*

    Salt to taste

    White pepper to taste

1½   *pounds cooked, drained, fresh green or lima beans (see page 15)*

Melt butter in medium-sized saucepan over medium heat. When melted, stir in flour. When combined, whisk in hot chicken stock until well incorporated. Then whisk in heavy cream, orange zest, basil, and salt and white pepper.

Lower heat and cook, stirring frequently, for about 5 minutes or until sauce is quite thick. Add the beans and cook for 2 minutes or until heated through. Serve immediately.

SESAME SNOW PEAS
SERVES 6

1½   *pounds snow peas, trimmed, or sugar snap peas*

2   *tablespoons soy sauce*

1   *teaspoon sesame oil*

1   *teaspoon peanut oil*

¼   *cup julienned water chestnuts*

1   *tablespoon toasted sesame seeds*

1   *teaspoon black sesame seeds*

Place snow peas in rapidly boiling water for about 30 seconds or until bright green and still crisp. Drain immediately and shock under cold running water. When well chilled, drain and pat dry.

Combine snow peas with remaining ingredients in medium-sized sauté pan over medium heat. Sauté for about 2 minutes or until just heated through. Serve immediately.

BEANS AGRO DOLCE
SERVES 6

¼   *cup clarified butter*

1   *tablespoon minced onions*

2   *tablespoons dried currants*

2   *tablespoons brown sugar*

3   *tablespoons balsamic vinegar*

3   *cups cooked, well-drained, dried or fresh beans of your choice (see page 15)*

Melt butter in heavy sauté pan over medium heat. When melted, add onions and sauté for 3 minutes. Stir in currants, brown sugar, and vinegar. Cook, stirring constantly, for about 4 minutes or until sugar has completely dissolved. Add beans. Lower heat to a minimum flame. Cover and cook for about 5 minutes.

Toss beans to coat. Taste. If the sweet/sour flavor seems well balanced, remove from heat. If not, add sugar or balsamic vinegar, whichever is necessary, a bit at a time, until balance is reached. Serve hot or at room temperature.

MINTED PEAS
SERVES 6

3   *tablespoons clarified butter*

1   *tablespoon chopped fresh mint, plus approximately 1 cup whole leaves*

4   *cups shelled fresh peas (or thawed frozen petite peas)*

¼   *cup chopped scallions*

Salt to taste

Pepper to taste

Heat butter in medium-sized saucepan over low heat. When melted, remove from heat and add chopped mint. Steep for about 15 minutes, keeping warm.

Place peas in top half of steamer. Cover with scallions and whole mint leaves. Place over rapidly boiling water and steam for 4 minutes or until peas are just tender. Remove from heat and discard whole mint leaves. Toss peas with mint butter, add salt and pepper, and serve immediately.

Minted Peas, a sophisticated accompaniment.

BEANS 'N GREENS

SERVES 6

2   *tablespoons clarified butter or vegetable oil*

1   *teaspoon minced fresh garlic*

1   *teaspoon minced fresh ginger*

¼   *cup minced fresh cilantro*

    or

2   *tablespoons olive oil*

1   *tablespoon minced garlic*

½   *teaspoon minced fresh oregano*

¼   *cup minced fresh Italian parsley*

    Add the following to either of the above:

2   *pounds fresh greens, washed and trimmed (mustard, collard, spinach, et cetera)*

3   *cups cooked, drained, dried beans or lentils (see page 15)*

    Salt to taste

    Pepper to taste

For either group of ingredients: Heat butter or oil in heavy sauté pan over medium heat. When hot, stir in garlic and seasonings and sauté for 3 minutes. Stir in greens. Cover and cook for about 4 minutes (depending on the green used) to wilt greens. Remove cover and stir in beans or lentils. Cook for 3 minutes or until beans are heated through. Add salt and pepper and serve hot.

BULGUR AND PEA PILAF

SERVES 6

1½   *cups bulgur wheat*

7   *cups boiling water*

2   *cups cooked fresh peas or beans (or cooked dried beans)*

½   *cup chopped scallions*

¼   *cup minced fresh cilantro*

½   *cup olive oil*

3   *tablespoons fresh lemon juice*

1   *tablespoon curry powder*

½   *teaspoon ground cumin*

½   *teaspoon ground turmeric*

    Dash cayenne

    Salt to taste

Place bulgur in large heatproof bowl and cover with boiling water. Cover and allow to stand for 2½ hours.

Pour into a fine sieve and let drain for 30 minutes. Place in a mixing bowl and combine with remaining ingredients. Let stand for about 30 minutes and serve at room temperature.

BOSTON BAKED BEANS

SERVES 6

4 cups dried navy or Great Northern beans

¾ cup maple syrup

¼ cup molasses

1 tablespoon dry mustard

Salt to taste

Pepper to taste

½ pound salt pork, cubed (optional)

Soak, rinse, and cook beans (see page 15). When cooked, drain well, reserving the liquid.

Preheat oven to 325°F.

Grease a 2-quart casserole or bean pot and set aside.

Combine drained beans with maple syrup, molasses, mustard, and salt and pepper. Stir in salt pork, if using. When well combined, taste and adjust seasonings by adding more sweetness or spice as desired. Stir in bean liquid to make beans quite soupy. If you do not have sufficient bean cooking liquid, use boiling water.

Pour into greased casserole and place in preheated oven. Cover and bake for about 4 hours, tasting frequently and adding liquid as necessary. When beans are very soft and the gravy is very thick and rich, beans are done. Uncover and let cook for another 20 minutes or until a crust forms on top. Remove from heat and serve hot.

GARLIC AND WHITE BEAN PUREE

SERVES 6

1 pound dried white kidney, Great Northern, fava, or navy beans

1 cup dry white wine

2 bulbs garlic, roasted and removed from skin

2 bay leaves

1 3-inch piece lemon peel

Salt to taste

Pepper to taste

½ cup extra virgin olive oil

Soak, rinse, and cook beans (see page 15). Thirty minutes before beans are done, stir in white wine, roasted garlic, bay leaves, lemon peel, and salt and pepper. When beans are very soft, remove from heat. Discard bay leaves and lemon peel and drain beans, reserving liquid.

Puree beans in food processor fitted with the metal blade, adding olive oil a bit at a time and adding reserved bean liquid, if necessary, to make a thick puree. When pureed, reheat in a saucepan over medium heat if serving hot.

FLORENTINE BEANS

SERVES 6

1   pound dried white beans

3   cloves garlic, peeled and chopped

1   teaspoon minced fresh sage

2   cups canned Italian plum tomatoes

     Salt to taste

     Pepper to taste

     Parmesan cheese to taste

Soak, rinse, and cook beans (see page 15). Set aside.

Heat oil in heavy saucepan over medium heat. When hot, add garlic and sage and cook, stirring frequently, for 4 minutes or until garlic begins to brown. Add beans, tomatoes, and salt and pepper and cook for about 30 minutes until quite thick. Remove from heat. Pour into a serving bowl and sprinkle with Parmesan cheese, if desired. Serve hot.

Variations:

1. Add ½ pound salt pork, cubed, to these beans and bake in a preheated 375°F oven for about 45 minutes.

2. Fresh lima beans, fava beans, or green beans may be substituted for dried beans. Adjust cooking time accordingly.

SOUR CREAM–BAKED LIMA BEANS

SERVES 6

1   pound dried lima beans or any dried bean of your
     choice

½   cup grated carrots

½   cup minced celery

1   tablespoon minced shallots

1   cup sour cream

2   tablespoons hot and sweet mustard

½   teaspoon minced fresh tarragon

     Salt to taste

     Pepper to taste

3   strips raw bacon (optional)

Soak, rinse, and cook beans (see page 15). When cooked, drain well.

Preheat oven to 375°F.

Combine beans with carrots, celery, shallots, sour cream, mustard, and tarragon. Add salt and pepper. Pour into a 2-quart casserole and, if using, place bacon strips on top. Place in preheated oven and bake for about 30 minutes or until bubbling. Serve hot.

Flavorful Florentine Beans.

CUBAN BLACK BEANS (MOORS AND CHRISTIANS)

SERVES 6

1	pound dried black beans
2	tablespoons vegetable oil
1	cup chopped onions
½	cup chopped red bell peppers
1	tablespoon minced garlic
1	cup peeled, cored, seeded, and chopped plum tomatoes
1	teaspoon ground cumin
¼	teaspoon cayenne (or to taste)
	Salt to taste
	Pepper to taste
2	cups long grain rice

Soak, rinse, and cook beans (see page 15). When cooked, drain beans, reserving liquid separately.

Heat oil in large saucepan over medium heat. When hot, add onions, bell peppers, and garlic. Sauté for 3 minutes or until onion is soft. Add tomatoes, cumin, cayenne, and salt and pepper and continue to cook for 10 minutes. Add beans with enough of the reserved liquid to make a thick gravy. Lower heat and simmer for 30 minutes, adding more liquid if necessary.

Cook rice as directed on package or by your usual method. When cooked, mound the rice (the Christians) in the center of a warm serving plate. Make a well in the center and spoon beans (the Moors) into it, allowing beans to spill out over the rice. Serve immediately.

CREAMED NEW POTATOES AND PEAS

SERVES 6

2	tablespoons unsalted butter
2	tablespoons all-purpose flour
1	cup warm milk
½	cup warm heavy cream
	Salt to taste
	White pepper to taste
½	cup chopped brie cheese, without rind
12	cooked tiny new potatoes
2	cups cooked, drained, fresh peas (see page 15)

Melt butter in a medium-sized saucepan over medium heat. When melted, stir in flour. When well combined, whisk in milk and cream. Cook, stirring constantly, for about 2 minutes or until sauce begins to thicken. Add salt and pepper and whisk in cheese. When cheese has melted, stir in potatoes and peas and cook for about 2 more minutes or until vegetables are heated through. Serve immediately.

This recipe is equally good made with sugar snap peas or fresh baby lima beans.

DAL PANCAKES

SERVES 6

1   cup pale yellow lentils or yellow split peas

½   cup vegetable broth

1   tablespoon minced fresh ginger

½   cup chopped onions

1   tablespoon minced fresh garlic

1   teaspoon minced fresh jalapeño pepper (or to taste)

¼   teaspoon ground cumin

¼   teaspoon ground turmeric

    Dash cinnamon

    Salt to taste

2   tablespoons minced fresh cilantro

1   tablespoon minced fresh parsley

1   tablespoon minced scallions

½   cup plain yogurt

¼   cup clarified butter

Soak the lentils in warm water to cover for 2 hours. Drain well.

Combine drained lentils, vegetable broth, ginger, onions, garlic, jalapeño pepper, spices, and salt in a food processor fitted with the metal blade. When well blended and frothy, pour into mixing bowl. Stir in cilantro, parsley, scallions, and ¼ cup yogurt.

Heat griddle over high heat. Coat with a thin layer of clarified butter. When griddle is hot, lower heat to medium-high and pour in enough batter to make a 5-inch pancake.

Cook for about 2 minutes or until underside is beginning to brown. Turn and cook other side for an additional 2 minutes. Continue cooking until all batter is used up, keeping finished pancakes warm. Serve warm with a dollop of yogurt.

HOPPIN' JOHN
SERVES 6

2   cups black-eyed peas, rinsed and drained

¾   pound salt pork, bacon, or ham

1   cup diced onions

1   cup long grain or brown rice

¼   teaspoon dried thyme

½   teaspoon red pepper flakes (or to taste)

     Salt to taste

     Pepper to taste

Place black-eyed peas with 8 cups of water in a deep saucepan over high heat. Bring to a boil, then lower heat and simmer, covered, for about 45 minutes or until the peas are tender but not mushy.

Cut the salt pork into ½-inch cubes. Place in a skillet over medium heat and fry for about 5 minutes or until crisp. Remove to a paper towel and drain well. Set aside.

Pour off all but 1 teaspoon bacon fat, then add the onions to the skillet. Place over medium heat and sauté, stirring frequently, for about 4 minutes or until just soft. Set aside.

When beans are done, ladle out all but 2½ cups cooking liquid.

Add rice, bacon, onions, thyme, red pepper flakes, and salt and pepper. Stir to combine.

Return to high heat and bring to a boil. Immediately lower heat and cover. Cook for about 25 minutes or until rice is done and liquid is absorbed. Turn off heat and let sit, covered, for 15 minutes. Serve with hot buttered cornbread, if desired.

There are as many versions of Hoppin' John as there are cooks. This traditional southern dish, served to welcome the new year, can be changed to incorporate collard greens, slices of meat, more onions, garlic, and hot seasonings. The rice can be cooked separately and combined with the peas at the last minute. This basic recipe should be your starting point!

JALAPEÑO BEANS
SERVES 6

4   cups cooked, drained, pigeon peas, or any cooked, dried or fresh bean of your choice (see page 15)

½   cup diced bell peppers

1   tablespoon fresh lime juice

2   fresh jalapeño peppers, sliced (or to taste)

1   teaspoon ground cumin

1   teaspoon maple syrup (or to taste)

     Salt to taste

     Pepper to taste

Combine all ingredients in a medium-sized saucepan over medium heat. Cook for about 5 minutes or until flavors have blended and beans are hot. Serve immediately or cover and refrigerate until ready to use, as this dish may be served hot or cold.

Hoppin' John, real comfort food on a cold winter night.

RED BEANS AND RICE
SERVES 6

1	pound dried red beans
3	tablespoons vegetable oil
1½	cups chopped onions
1	cup chopped green bell peppers
1	cup chopped celery
2	tablespoons minced garlic
1	cup peeled, cored, seeded, and chopped tomatoes
1	teaspoon dried oregano
½	teaspoon dried thyme
3	bay leaves
1	teaspoon paprika
½	teaspoon cayenne
½	teaspoon ground cumin
¼	cup vinegar
1	teaspoon Tabasco (or to taste)
	Red pepper flakes to taste
	Salt to taste
	Pepper to taste
1½	cups long grain rice

Soak, rinse, and cook beans (see page 15).

Heat oil in heavy sauté pan over medium heat. When hot, add onions, bell pepper, celery, and garlic and sauté for 3 minutes or until vegetables begin to soften. Stir in tomatoes, herbs, spices, and vinegar. Cook for about 15 minutes or until vegetables are tender. Scrape into beans. Add Tabasco, red pepper flakes, and salt and pepper. Place beans over medium heat and cook for 10 minutes or until heated through.

Cook rice as directed on package or by your usual method. When cooked, place in a deep serving bowl and pour beans over top. Pass additional Tabasco and white vinegar if desired.

REFRIED BEANS

SERVES 6

1   *pound dried pinto or pink beans*

1   *cup diced onions*

1   *tablespoon minced garlic*

1   *teaspoon minced fresh epazote (optional)*

     Salt to taste

     Pepper to taste

1   *cup bacon fat or vegetable oil*

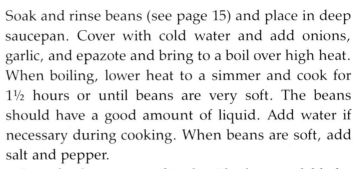

Soak and rinse beans (see page 15) and place in deep saucepan. Cover with cold water and add onions, garlic, and epazote and bring to a boil over high heat. When boiling, lower heat to a simmer and cook for 1½ hours or until beans are very soft. The beans should have a good amount of liquid. Add water if necessary during cooking. When beans are soft, add salt and pepper.

In a food processor fitted with the metal blade, mash the beans with their liquid, but do not puree. Beans should be a bit chunky.

Heat ½ cup bacon fat or oil in a heavy sauté pan over medium-high heat. Add mashed beans and cook, stirring constantly, for about 15 minutes, incorporating the oil into the beans and cooking until the beans are almost dry. Allow beans to cool, then repeat process using remaining oil, incorporating 2 tablespoons at a time into the beans until they are very hot. You may not need to use all of the remaining bacon fat or oil.

Variations:

1. When frying beans for the first time, you may add onion, garlic, and tomato, if desired.

2. You can also incorporate 2 cups shredded queso blanco or Monterey Jack cheese just before serving.

CHAPTER SIX

MISCELLANEOUS

CECI ❦ BEAN PIE ❦ FALAFEL

BEAN PIZZA ❦ FERMENTED BLACK BEAN SAUCE

MEDITERRANEAN BEAN SAUCE

Ceci

Serves 6

1	pound dried chick-peas
½	cup unsalted butter
2	tablespoons vegetable oil
1	tablespoon minced garlic
	with
2	tablespoons chili powder
1	teaspoon ground cumin
¼	teaspoon cayenne
	Salt to taste
	or
2	tablespoons curry powder
1	teaspoon ground coriander
½	teaspoon ground cumin
½	teaspoon ground ginger
	Salt to taste
	Or any combination of herbs and spices

Soak, rinse, and cook chick-peas (see page 15). Do not allow beans to get too soft. When tender but still firm, remove from heat and drain well. Pat dry.

Preheat oven to 375°F.

Melt butter in medium-sized saucepan over low heat. Add vegetable oil and garlic and allow to sit for 5 minutes, keeping warm.

Pour butter into large baking tray with sides. Spread dried chick-peas on tray. Bake 15 minutes, turning frequently, or until chick-peas are golden.

While chick-peas are baking, combine spices and herbs. When chick-peas are done, remove from oven and sprinkle with herbs and spices and toss to coat. Serve warm.

Bean Pie

Makes 1 9-inch pie

3	cups dried, cooked, mashed, beans of choice (page 15)
3	large eggs
¾	cup melted unsalted butter
1	tablespoon cornstarch
1	teaspoon ground cinnamon
1	teaspoon ground ginger
½	teaspoon ground cloves
1	tablespoon fresh lemon (or orange) juice
1	cup evaporated milk
1	cup brown sugar (for dessert pie), or
2	tablespoons honey (for side dish)
1	unbaked pie shell

Preheat oven to 450°F.

Combine all ingredients except pie shell. Stir to blend. When well combined, pour into pie shell. Place in preheated oven and bake for 15 minutes. Lower heat to 350°F and bake for an additional 30 minutes or until center is set.

As stated in the list of ingredients, bean pie may be used as either a dessert pie or a side dish. If using as a dessert pie, it can be enhanced with a dollop of freshly whipped cream.

Ceci, garnished with red onion slices.

FALAFEL

SERVES 6 TO 8

3   *cups cooked, drained, chick-peas*

1   *cup chopped onions*

1   *teaspoon minced garlic*

½   *cup chopped fresh Italian parsley*

1   *teaspoon minced jalapeño pepper (or to taste)*

1   *teaspoon ground cumin*

1   *teaspoon baking powder*

    Salt to taste

    Pepper to taste

    Approximately 4 cups vegetable oil

6   *warm whole-wheat pitas*

2   *cups shredded iceberg lettuce*

    Tahini Sauce*

Combine chick-peas, onions, garlic, parsley, cilantro, jalapeño pepper, cumin, baking powder, and salt and pepper in food processor fitted with the metal blade, using quick on-and-off turns. Do not puree. Cover and refrigerate for 30 minutes.

When chilled, form chick-pea mixture into patties 2 inches round and about ¾ of an inch thick. Set aside.

Heat oil in deep-sided frying pan over high heat. When hot, carefully lower patties into hot oil a few at a time using a slotted spoon. Fry for about 3 minutes, turning frequently, until patties are golden. Drain on a paper towel.

Cut pitas in half. Place two falafel in each pocket and sprinkle with lettuce and drizzle with Tahini Sauce*.

TAHINI SAUCE

MAKES APPROXIMATELY 1½ CUPS OF SAUCE

1   *cup tahini (sesame seed paste)*

    Juice of 2 lemons

2   *cloves garlic, peeled*

    Salt to taste

    Approximately ½ cup cool water

Place tahini, lemon juice, garlic, and salt in food processor fitted with the metal blade. Process until smooth, adding enough water to make a thin sauce. Cover and refrigerate until ready to use.

Falafel with Tahini Sauce, a vegetarian delight!

BEAN PIZZA

SERVES 6

12   *pita breads*

3   *tablespoons olive oil*

1   *cup chopped onions*

1   *teaspoon minced garlic*

¼   *cup minced fresh Italian parsley*

4   *cups dried, cooked, drained beans: chick-peas,
        cannellini, kidney, black, or a combination, chopped*

1   *tablespoon minced fresh basil*

½   *teaspoon minced fresh oregano*

      Tabasco to taste

3   *large ripe tomatoes, cored and thinly sliced*

2½   *cups shredded smoked mozzarella cheese*

1   *cup grated Parmesan cheese*

Preheat broiler.

Carefully split pita bread. Brush with 2 tablespoons olive oil and place under preheated broiler for 2 minutes or until just brown. Remove and set aside.

Set oven to 375°F.

Heat remaining oil in heavy sauté pan over medium heat. Add onions, garlic, and parsley. Sauté until vegetables are just soft. Stir in beans, herbs, and Tabasco. Lower heat and cook for about 5 minutes.

Spread beans over the top of each toasted pita. Cover with the sliced tomatoes, then sprinkle generously with shredded mozzarella and then with grated Parmesan. Place on a baking sheet and bake in a preheated oven for 10 minutes or until hot and bubbly. Serve warm.

FERMENTED BLACK BEAN SAUCE

MAKES 2 CUPS

¼   cup peanut oil

½   cup chopped onions

¼   cup minced red bell peppers

1   teaspoon minced garlic

1   tablespoon minced fresh ginger

1   red hot chili pepper, seeded and minced

¼   cup fermented black beans, rinsed, drained, and dried
       (Available from Asian markets, specialty stores,
       and some supermarkets.)

2   tablespoons dry sherry

3   tablespoons sweet soy sauce (Available from Asian
       markets, specialty stores, and some supermarkets.)
       or 2 tablespoons soy sauce plus ½ teaspoon dark
       brown sugar

1½   cups chicken stock

1   teaspoon cornstarch (optional)

Heat oil in a heavy sauté pan over medium heat. When hot, add onions, bell pepper, garlic, ginger, and chili pepper. Sauté for 3 minutes or until vegetables are soft. Add black beans and stir, pushing on beans to slightly mash them. Add remaining ingredients except cornstarch, and simmer for about 10 minutes. If sauce needs thickening, dissolve cornstarch in 1 teaspoon cold water and stir into the sauce a bit at a time. Serve warm over vegetables or rice noodles or as a dipping sauce for crudités.

MEDITERRANEAN BEAN SAUCE

MAKES APPROXIMATELY 2 CUPS

1½   cups drained, cooked white beans (see page 15)

¼   cup diced, seedless, skinless tomatoes

2   tablespoons roasted fresh garlic

1   tablespoon minced shallots

1   tablespoon minced fresh parsley

1   6-ounce jar roasted sweet red peppers, well-drained

⅓   cup olive oil

       Salt to taste

       White pepper to taste

Combine beans, tomatoes, garlic, shallots, and parsley in a food processor fitted with the metal blade. When well blended, add peppers and process until smooth.

With the motor running, add the olive oil in a steady stream. Blend for about 30 seconds or until a thick sauce is formed. Remove from processor bowl. Season to taste with salt and pepper.

This sauce can be used on steamed vegetables, grilled or baked poultry, fish, or shellfish, or as a dip for crudités and chips.

KITCHEN METRICS

The table gives approximate, rather than exact, conversions.

SPOONS

¼ teaspoon	=	1	milliliter
½ teaspoon	=	2	milliliters
1 teaspoon	=	5	milliliters
1 tablespoon	=	15	milliliters
2 tablespoons	=	25	milliliters
3 tablespoons	=	50	milliliters

CUPS

¼ cup	=	50 milliliters
⅓ cup	=	75 milliliters
½ cup	=	125 milliliters
⅔ cup	=	150 milliliters
¾ cup	=	175 milliliters
1 cup	=	250 milliliters

OVEN TEMPERATURES

200°F	= 100°C
225°F	= 110°C
250°F	= 120°C
275°F	= 140°C
300°F	= 150°C
325°F	= 160°C
350°F	= 180°C
375°F	= 190°C
400°F	= 200°C
425°F	= 220°C
450°F	= 230°C
475°F	= 240°C

We gratefully acknowledge the assistance of the following manufacturers and merchants in providing us with the props and accessories used in this book.

FF   FITZ AND FLOYD, INC.
       2055-C Luna Road
       Carrollton, TX 75006

Z   ZONA
       97 Greene Street
       New York, NY 10012

ABC ABC CARPET AND HOME
       888 Broadway
       New York, NY 10003
       Loren Pack, 473-3000

PB   POTTERY BARN
       700 Broadway
       New York, NY 10003

B   BENNINGTON POTTERS, INC.
       P.O. Box 199
       Bennington, VT 05201

23:plate-FF,fork-PB,napkin-ABC;
29:plate-FF;
41:plate-PB,glass bowl-Z;
47:plate-PB,ladle-Z;
52:candlestick and placemat-PB;
58:plate-FF;
63:plate-PB;
69:plate-FF,napkin-ABC;
83:plate-FF,napkin-ABC;
90:plate-FF,flatware-PB;
94:candlestick and flatware-PB;
101:plate-FF,all else-PB;
105:plate-FF;
108:all-PB;
113:souffle-B, cloth - ABC;
119:all-PB;
121:plate-PB.

Thanks to Dean and DeLuca for providing some of the more unusual beans   Prop Styling by Heidi Carlson